Elsewhere

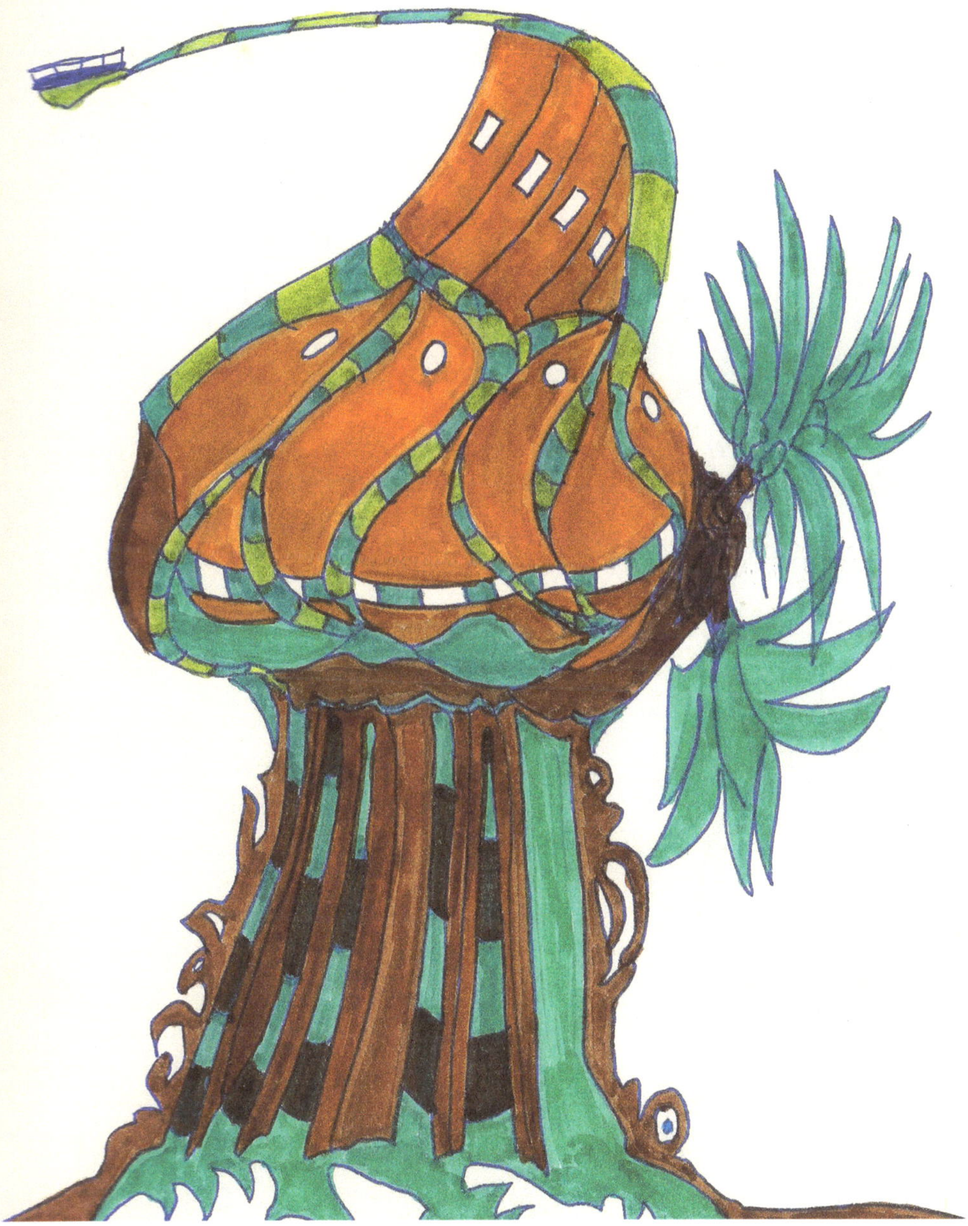

Printed in the United States of America

First Edition 2014

Scurfpea Publishing
P.O. Box 46
Sioux Falls, SD 57101
scurfpeapublishing.com
editor@scurfpeapublishing.com

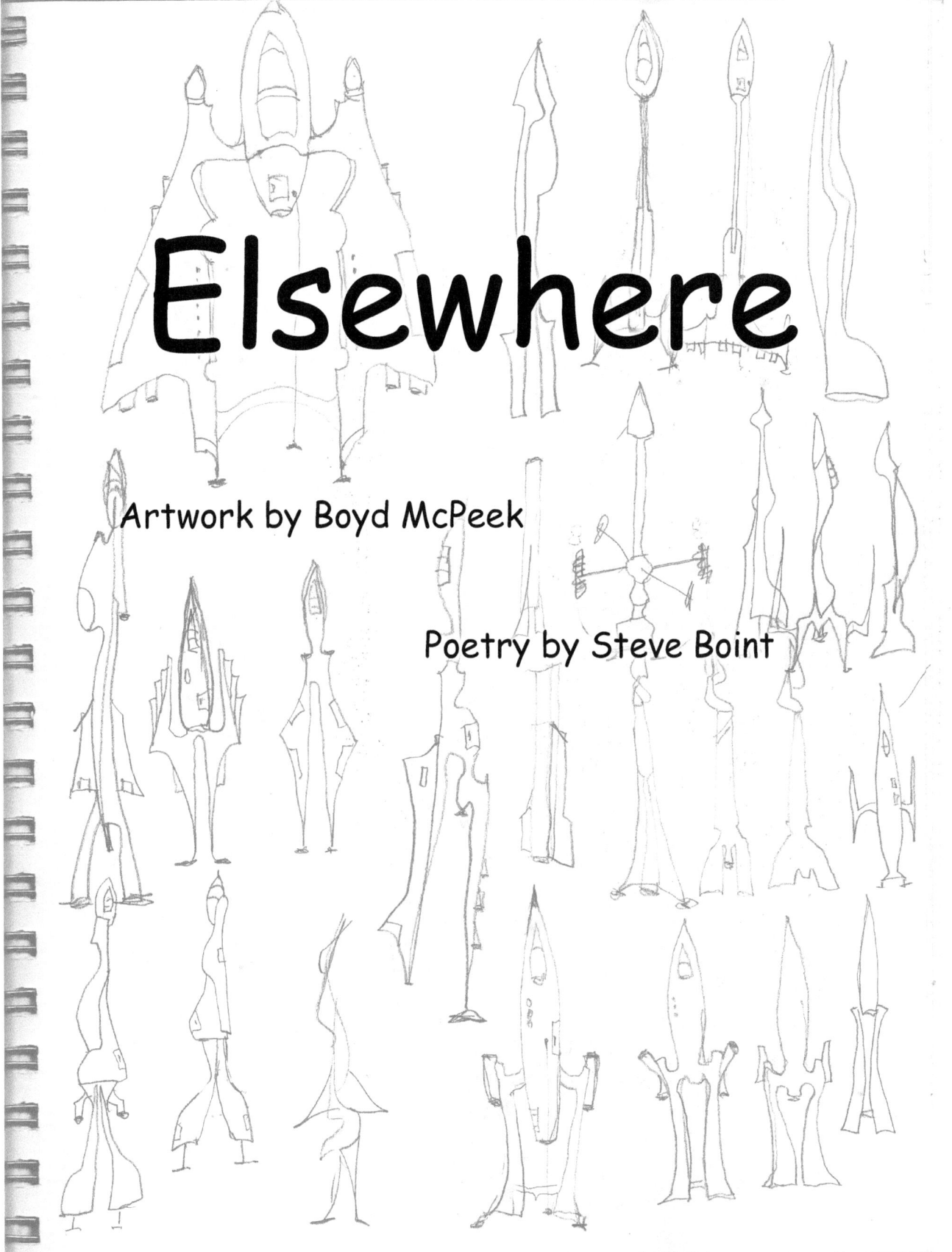

Elsewhere

Artwork by Boyd McPeek

Poetry by Steve Boint

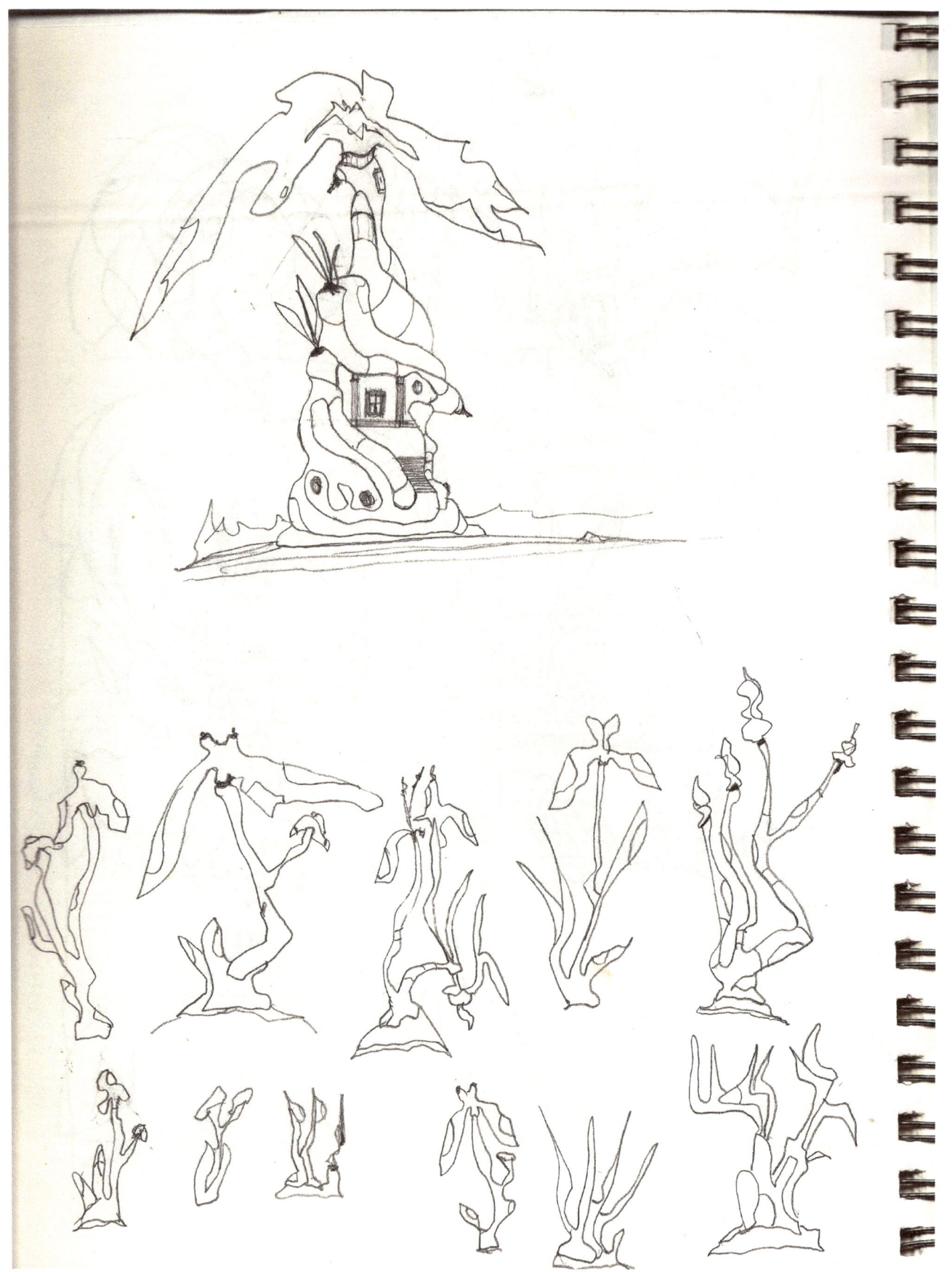

iv

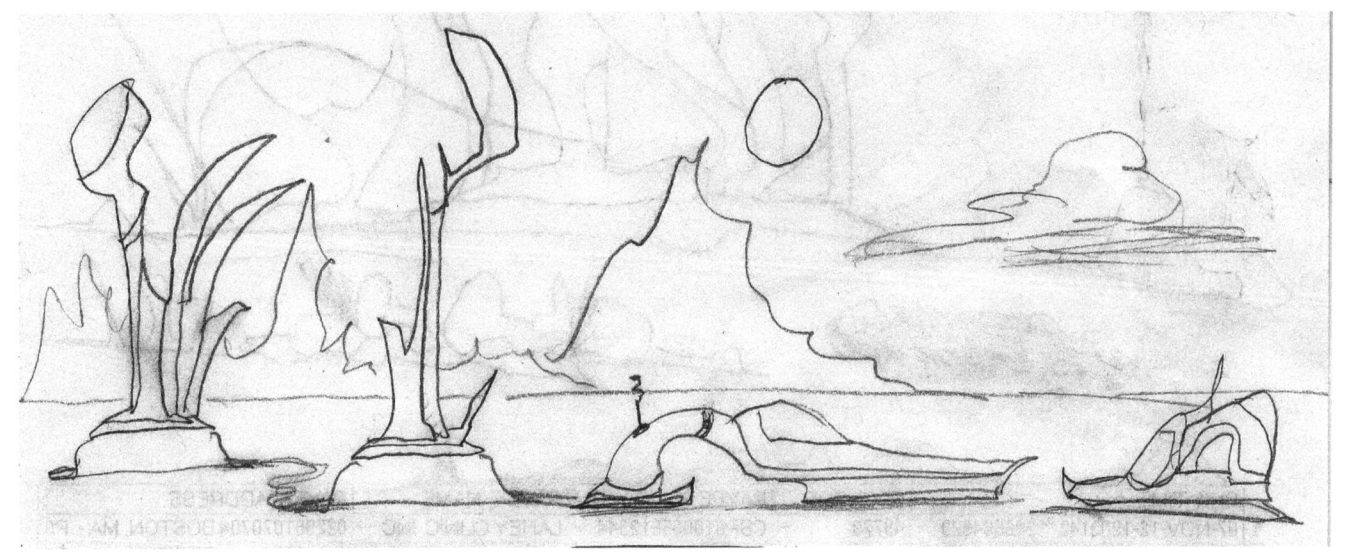

Contents

Pages from Boyd McPeek's notebook are reproduced in the beginning and end matter.

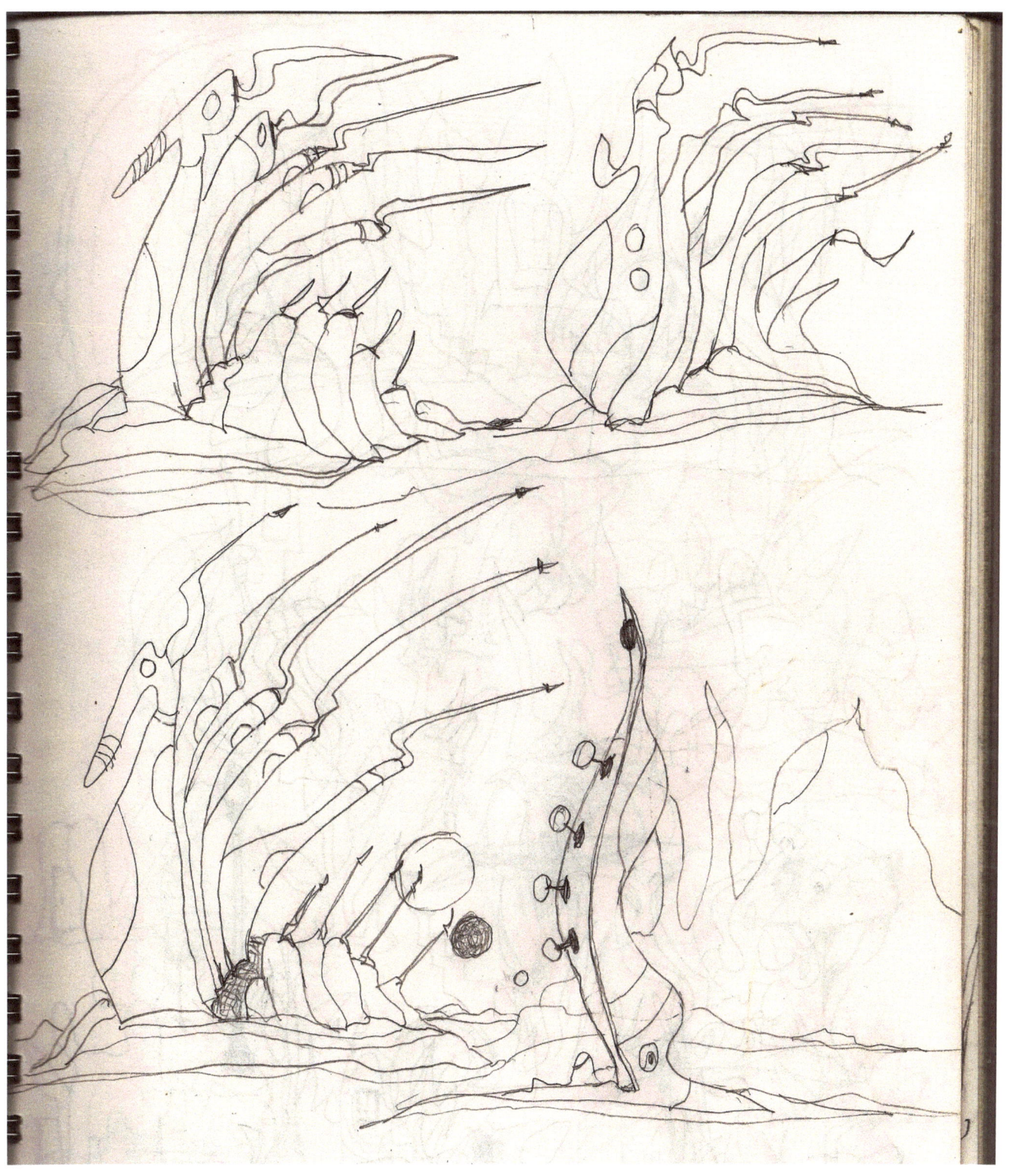

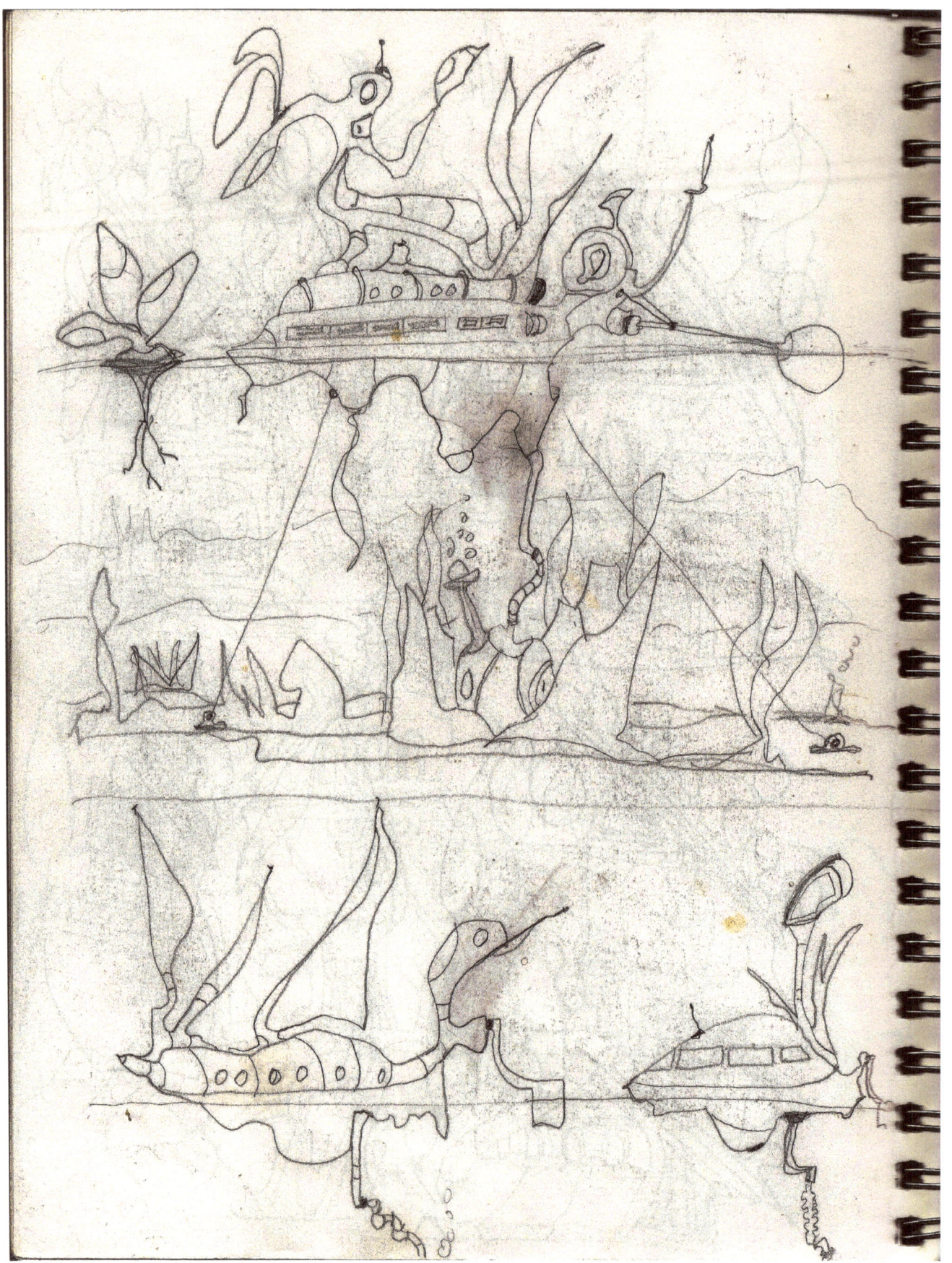

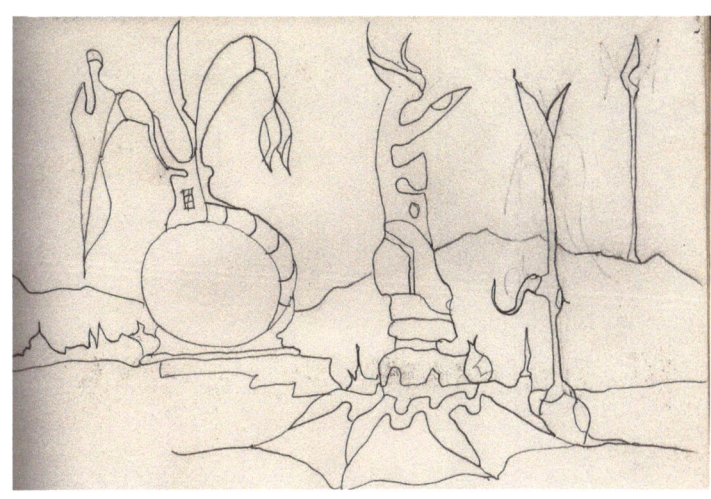

Foreword

It all started with *Rocket Girl* penned and emailed to a couple of friends, one of whom was Boyd. To my delight, over coffee two weeks later, on the wobbly table between us, he dropped the poem accompanied by artwork it currently adorns. Before long, we were sending poems and images back and forth.

Usually, Boyd would email me a graphic or five. I would toy with the images, attempting to capture their feel in words; but not the feel I felt he intended. I wanted to give each a twist which would surprise him. Quite often, the surprise wasn't pleasant—as our many abandoned attempts testify. This book contains those collaborations which we both felt worked well.

Over the several years of accumulation involved in this book, Boyd and I were both going through personal and professional struggles. For me, his happy worlds were vacations I would like to take, places I would like to see. They gave me a happy place when one was desperately needed. They were my elsewhere.

While these pieces should be read and viewed as separate snippets of worlds out there somewhere, short stand-alone pieces that invite the mind to wander, they are not without social relevance. Boyd's world of organic technology mirrors his firm commitment to environmentalism and a waste-not way of life. They mirror his love for this planet. They mirror his unique backyard. They also house his ability to celebrate the peace and quirkiness available in life. I'm a bit more of a brooder and this shows in my work. Recurrent themes include: the dangers of global ecological disaster, the waste of war, the limits as well as benefits of science, the value of oddball people, and the wisdom of placing relationships above achievement. But, for both of us, the main point was having fun and we hope you do too.

So, hop into your imagination and join us on a journey or three elsewhere.

x

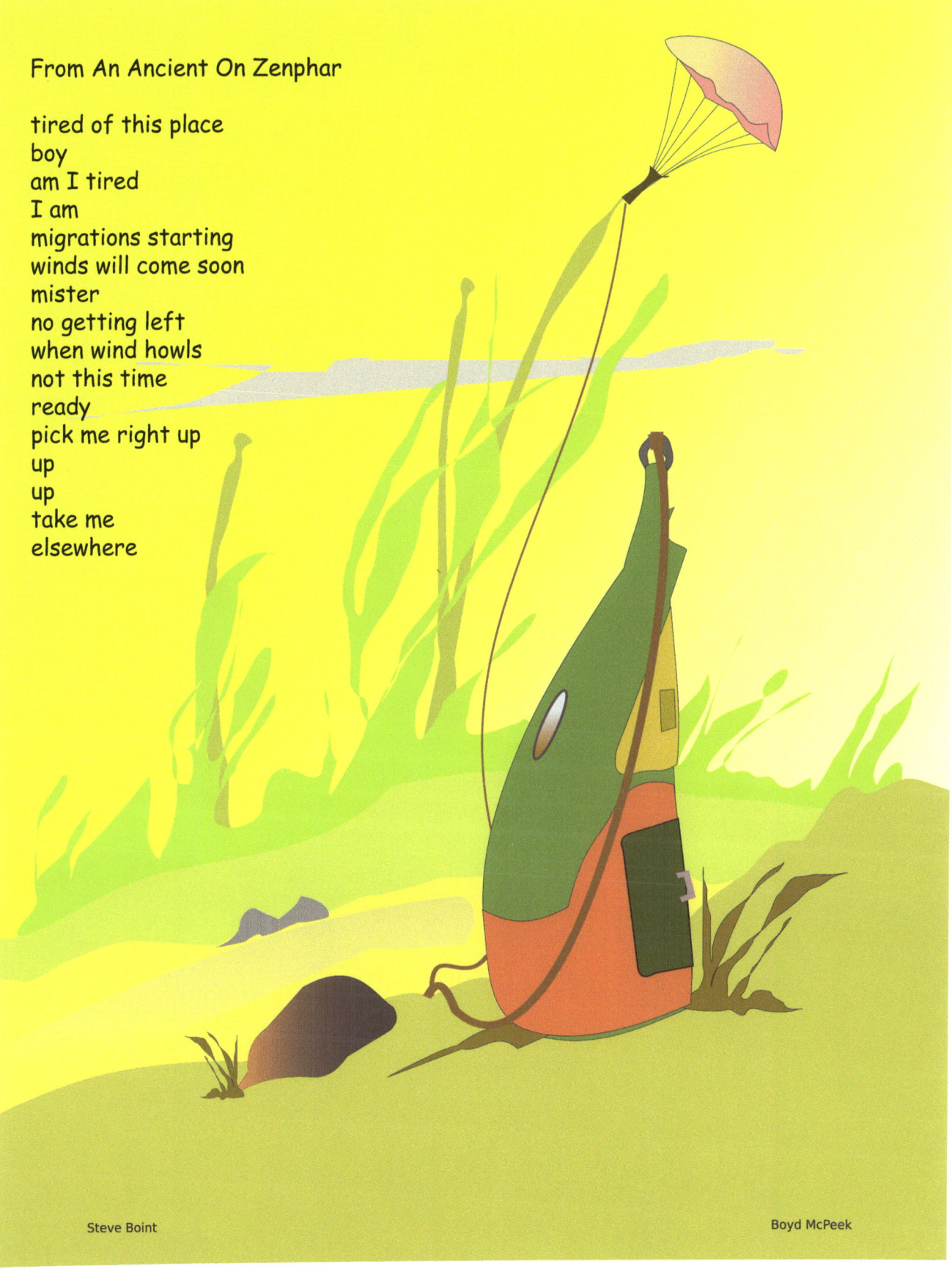

From An Ancient On Zenphar

tired of this place
boy
am I tired
I am
migrations starting
winds will come soon
mister
no getting left
when wind howls
not this time
ready
pick me right up
up
up
take me
elsewhere

Steve Boint

Boyd McPeek

1

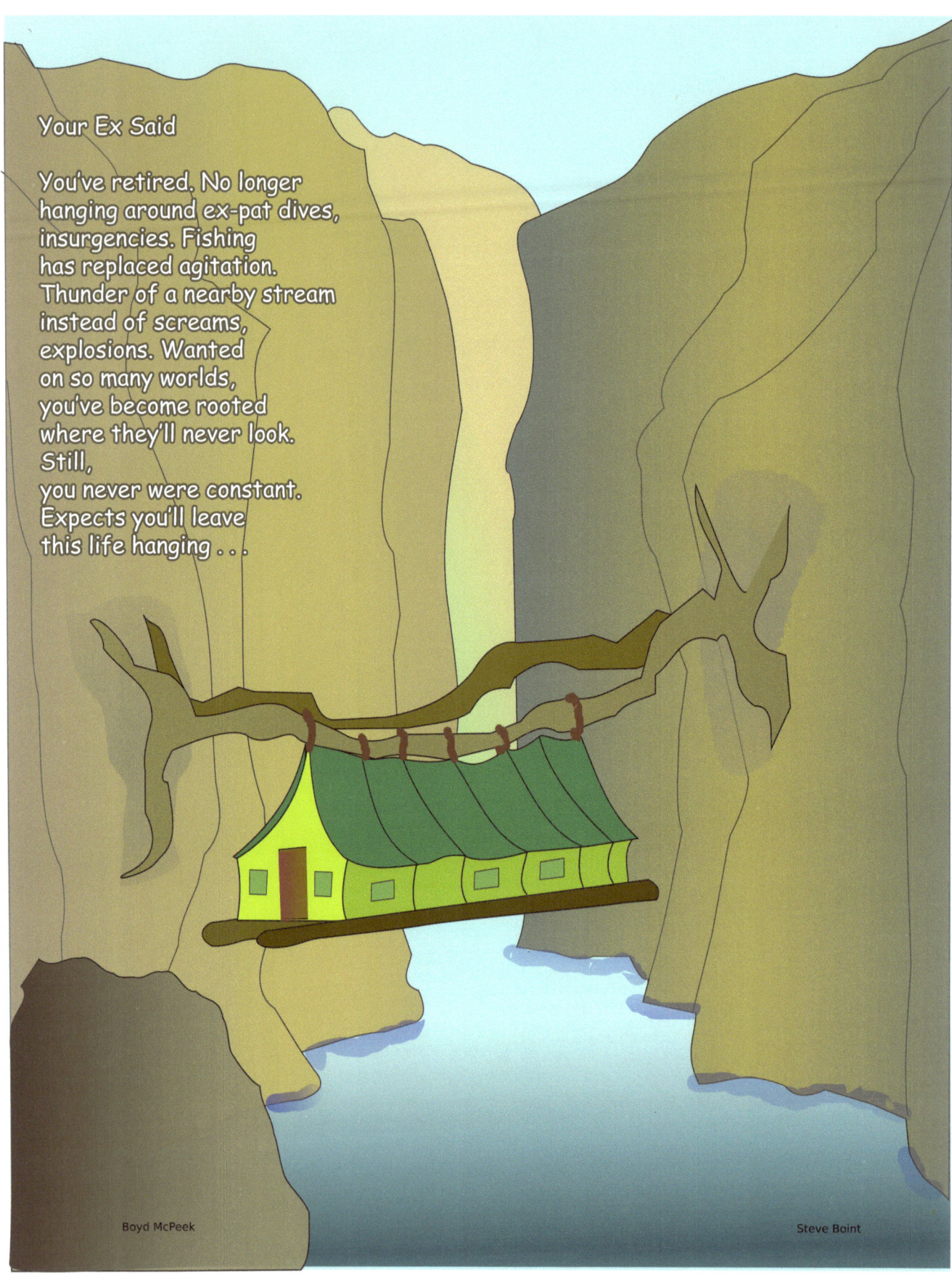

Your Ex Said

You've retired. No longer
hanging around ex-pat dives,
insurgencies. Fishing
has replaced agitation.
Thunder of a nearby stream
instead of screams,
explosions. Wanted
on so many worlds,
you've become rooted
where they'll never look.
Still,
you never were constant.
Expects you'll leave
this life hanging . . .

Boyd McPeek   Steve Boint

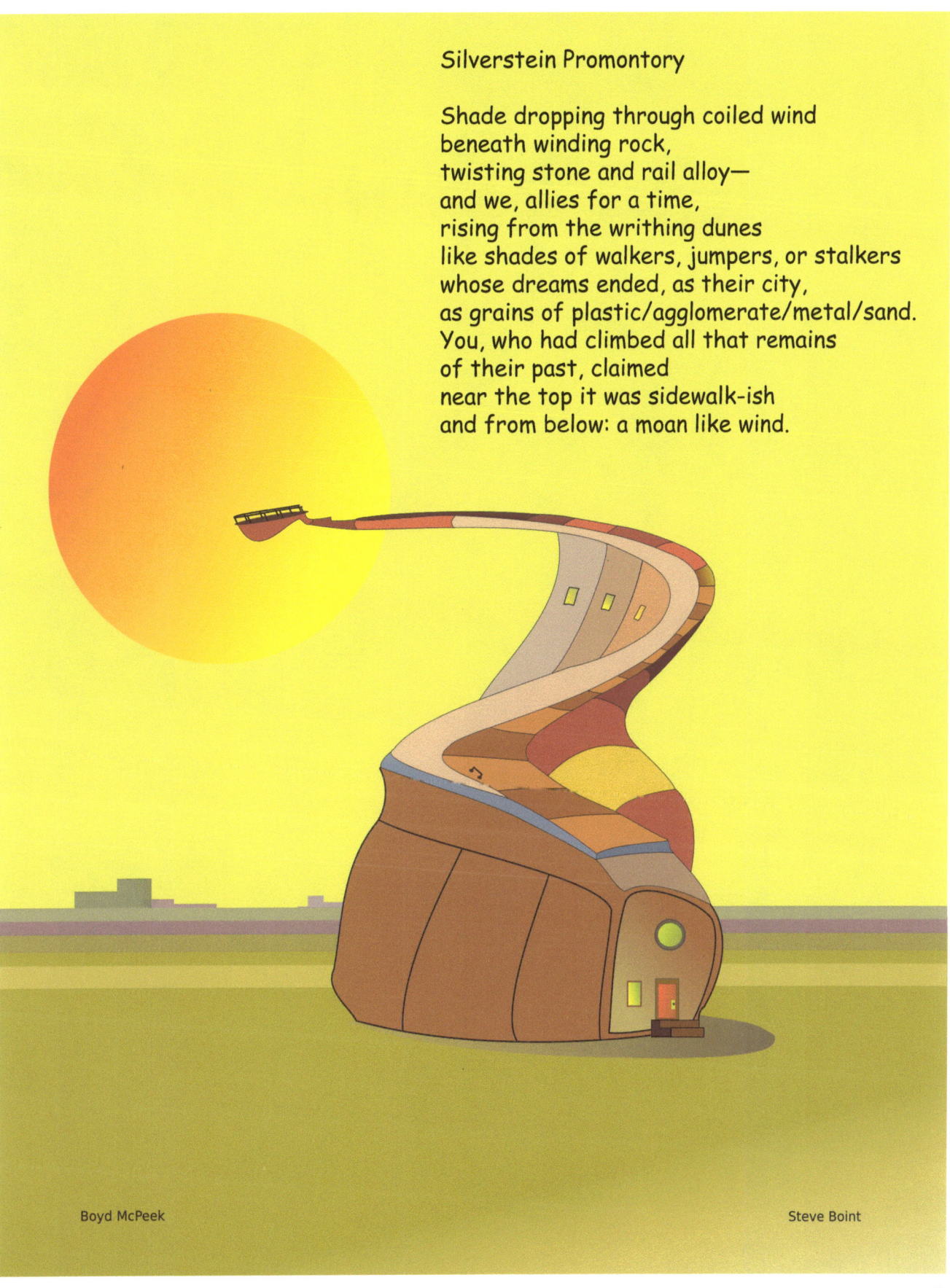

Silverstein Promontory

Shade dropping through coiled wind
beneath winding rock,
twisting stone and rail alloy—
and we, allies for a time,
rising from the writhing dunes
like shades of walkers, jumpers, or stalkers
whose dreams ended, as their city,
as grains of plastic/agglomerate/metal/sand.
You, who had climbed all that remains
of their past, claimed
near the top it was sidewalk-ish
and from below: a moan like wind.

Boyd McPeek

Steve Boint

something's happening
air fills me
lifting
lifting
this is flying
rising
rising
there's my family by the door
waving
waving
mom shoves my sister off

Steve Boint

plunging
plunging
plunging
growing dark
alone
air is thicker
strange smells
strange sounds
let go

give up hope

falling
falling
falling
past neighbors and houses

Boyd McPeek

4

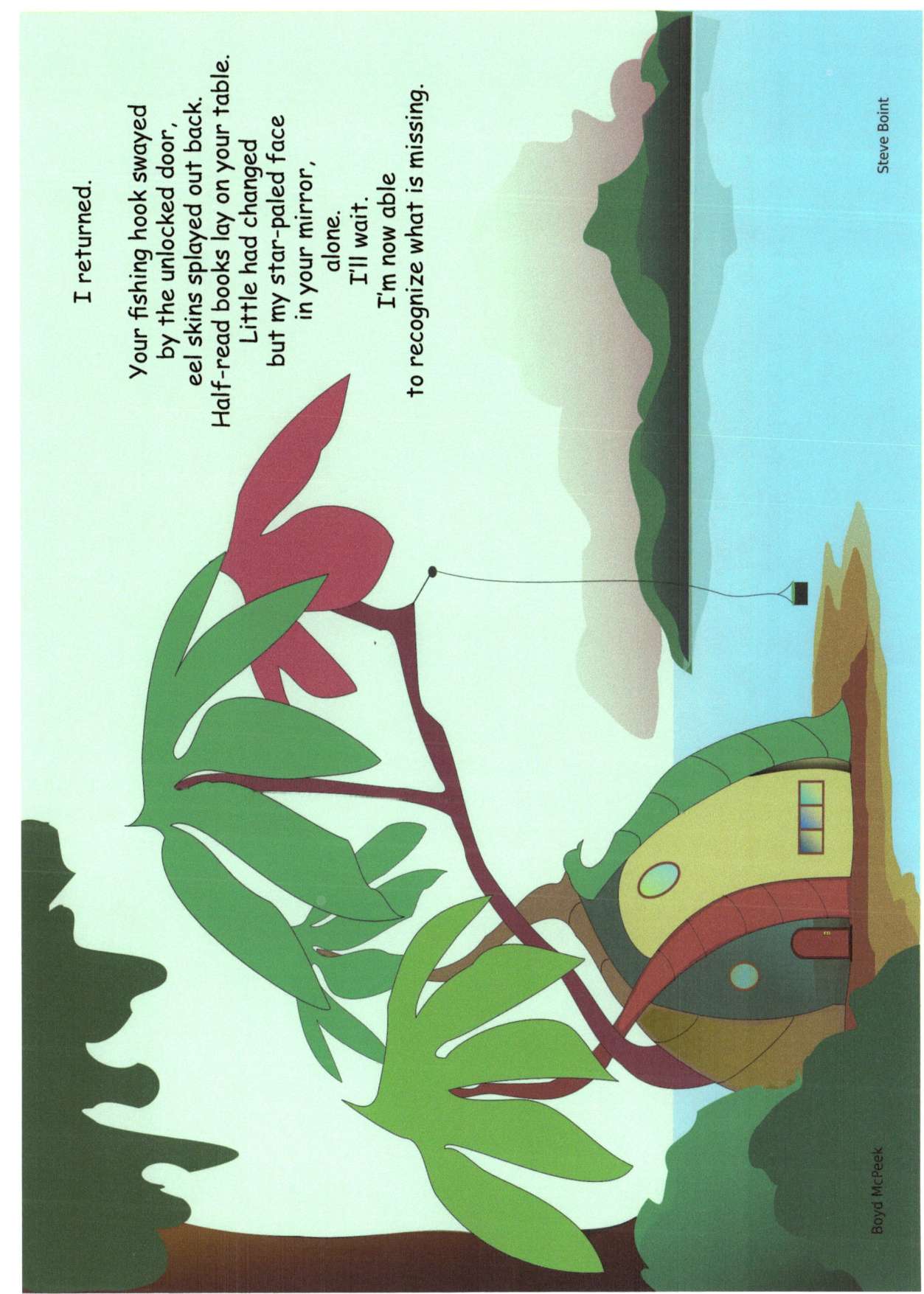

I returned.

Your fishing hook swayed
by the unlocked door,
eel skins splayed out back.
Half-read books lay on your table.
Little had changed
but my star-paled face
in your mirror,
alone.
I'll wait.
I'm now able
to recognize what is missing.

Steve Boint

Boyd McPeek

5

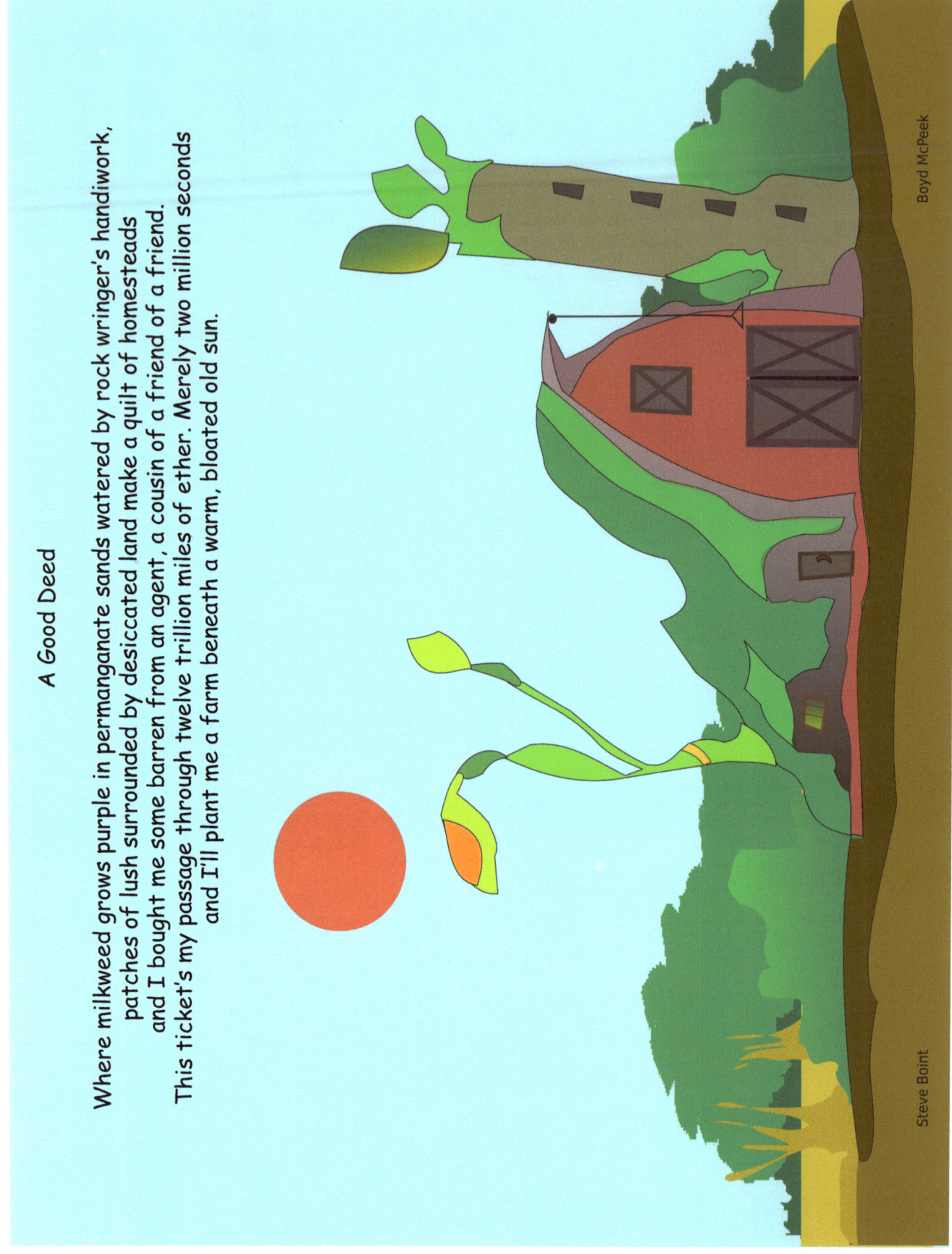

A Good Deed

Where milkweed grows purple in permanganate sands watered by rock wringer's handiwork,
patches of lush surrounded by desiccated land make a quilt of homesteads
and I bought me some barren from an agent, a cousin of a friend of a friend.
This ticket's my passage through twelve trillion miles of ether. Merely two million seconds
and I'll plant me a farm beneath a warm, bloated old sun.

Steve Boint

Boyd McPeek

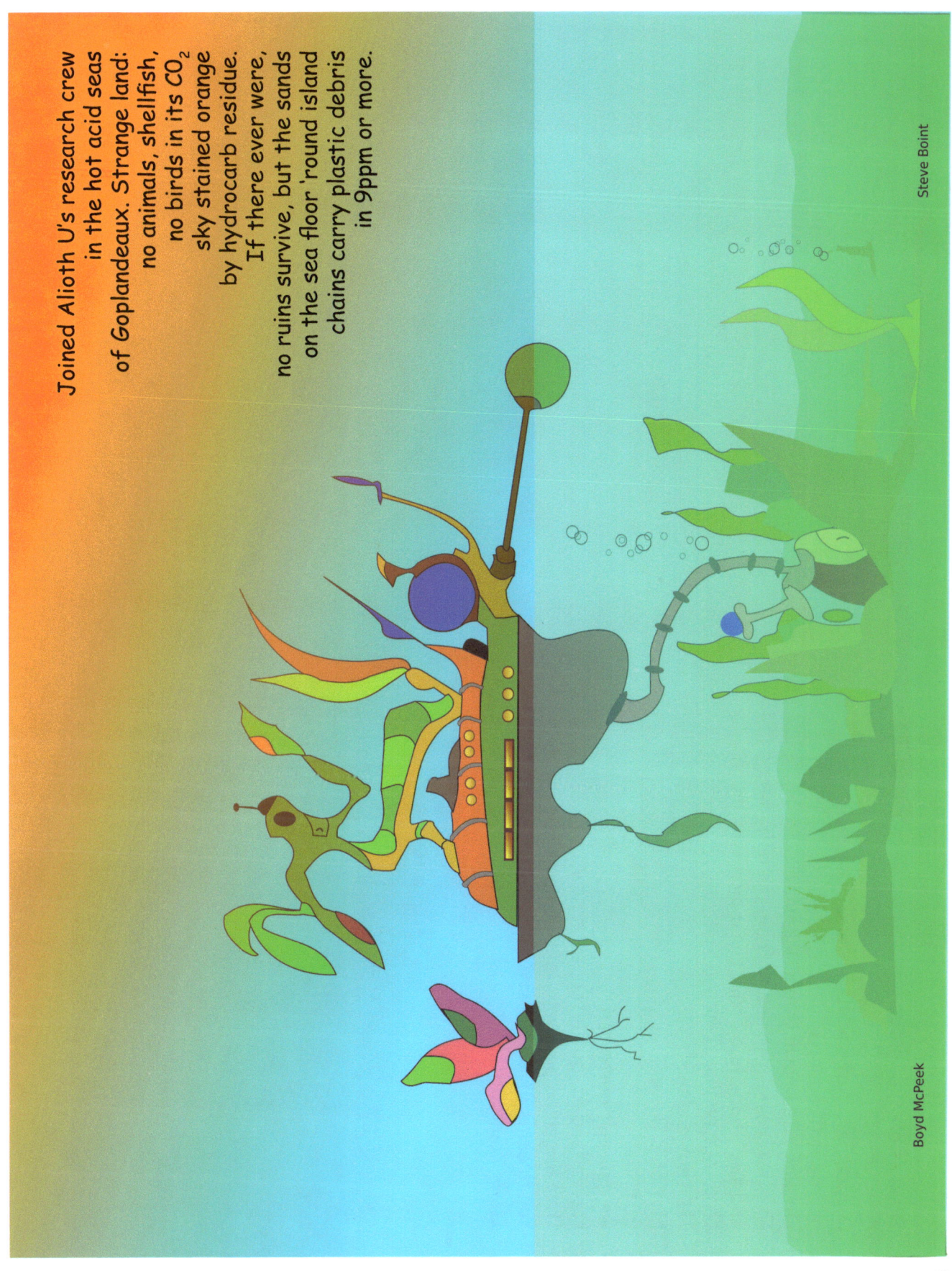

Joined Alioth U's research crew
in the hot acid seas
of Goplandeaux. Strange land:
no animals, shellfish,
no birds in its CO_2
sky stained orange
by hydrocarb residue.
If there ever were,
no ruins survive, but the sands
on the sea floor 'round island
chains carry plastic debris
in 9ppm or more.

Steve Boint

Boyd McPeek

7

Discretion Half-Regretted

Remember that strange island flower
on the water moon
circling the brown dwarf V'louer?
Exotic/erotic, the scent from its half-opened bloom
and the shore had room for a picnic or more.
Over our engine, I heard you yell,
"Is that a claw?"
Not on a flower.
But . . . .
we couldn't quite tell.
Never landed, but later, even now,
that lingering perfume left no room
for dreams of elsewhere.
If we could bottle it . . . .

Steve Boint

Boyd McPeek

8

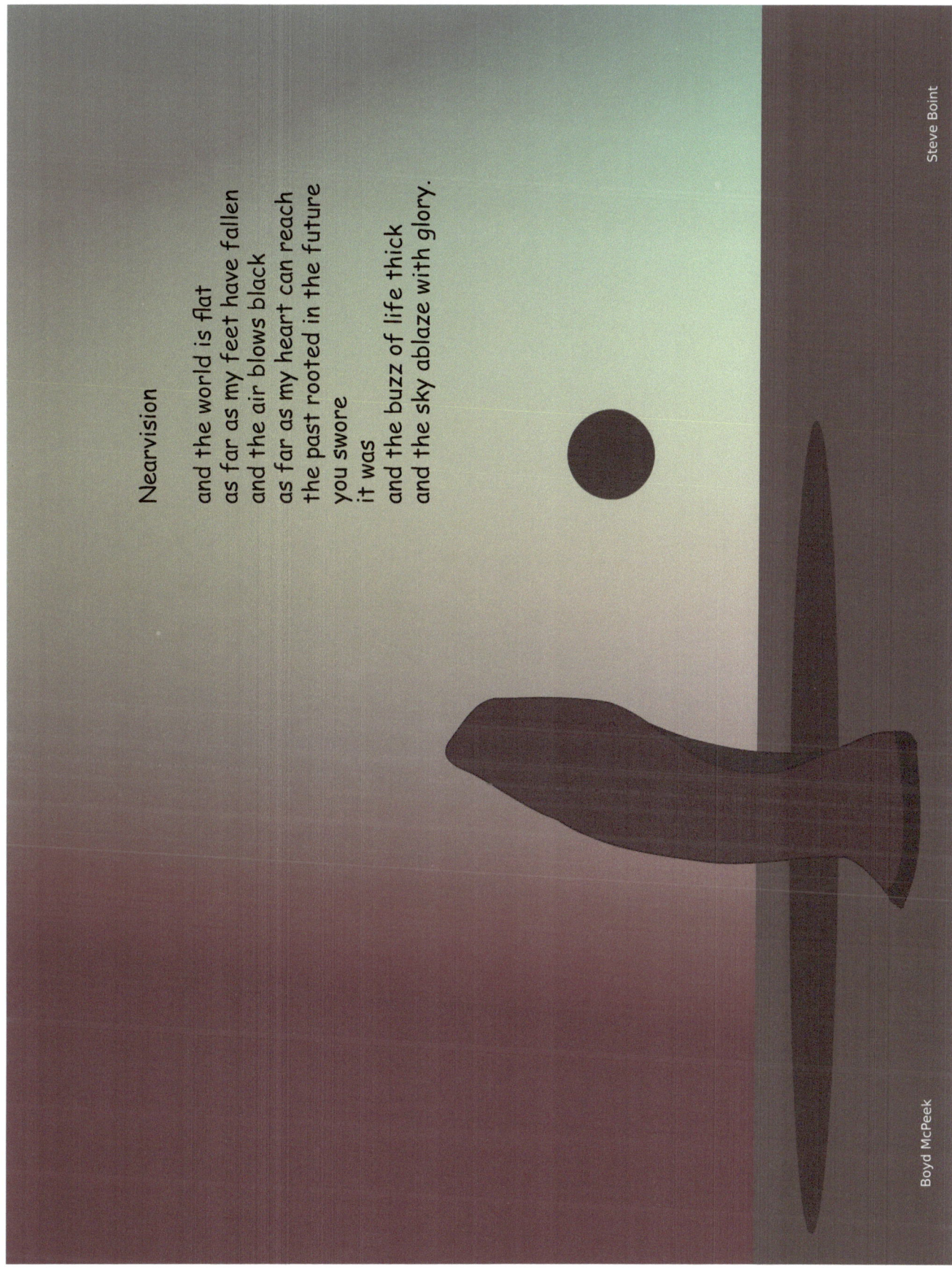

Nearvision

and the world is flat
as far as my feet have fallen
and the air blows black
as far as my heart can reach
the past rooted in the future
you swore
it was
and the buzz of life thick
and the sky ablaze with glory.

Steve Boint

Boyd McPeek

9

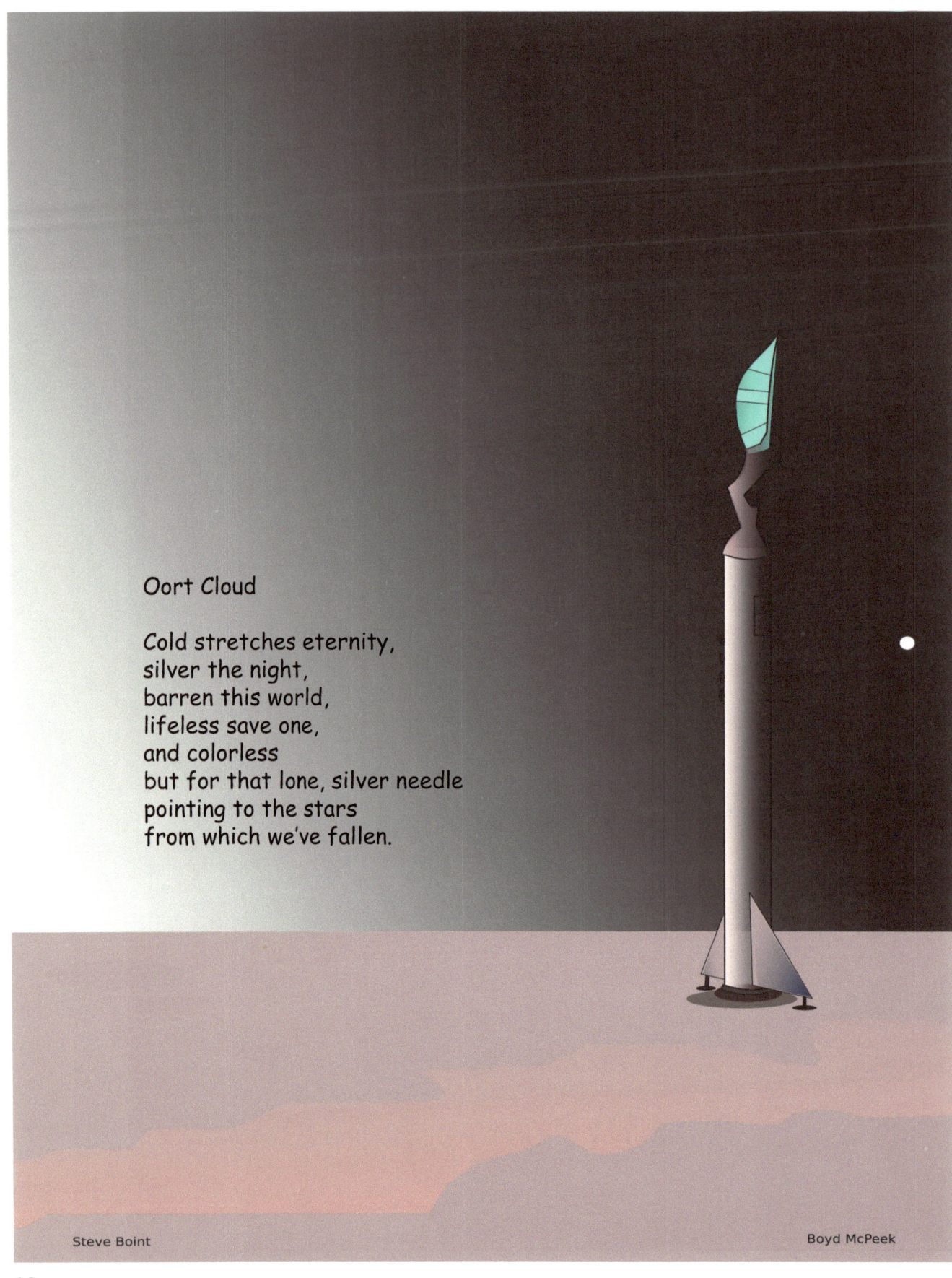

Oort Cloud

Cold stretches eternity,
silver the night,
barren this world,
lifeless save one,
and colorless
but for that lone, silver needle
pointing to the stars
from which we've fallen.

Steve Boint

Boyd McPeek

10

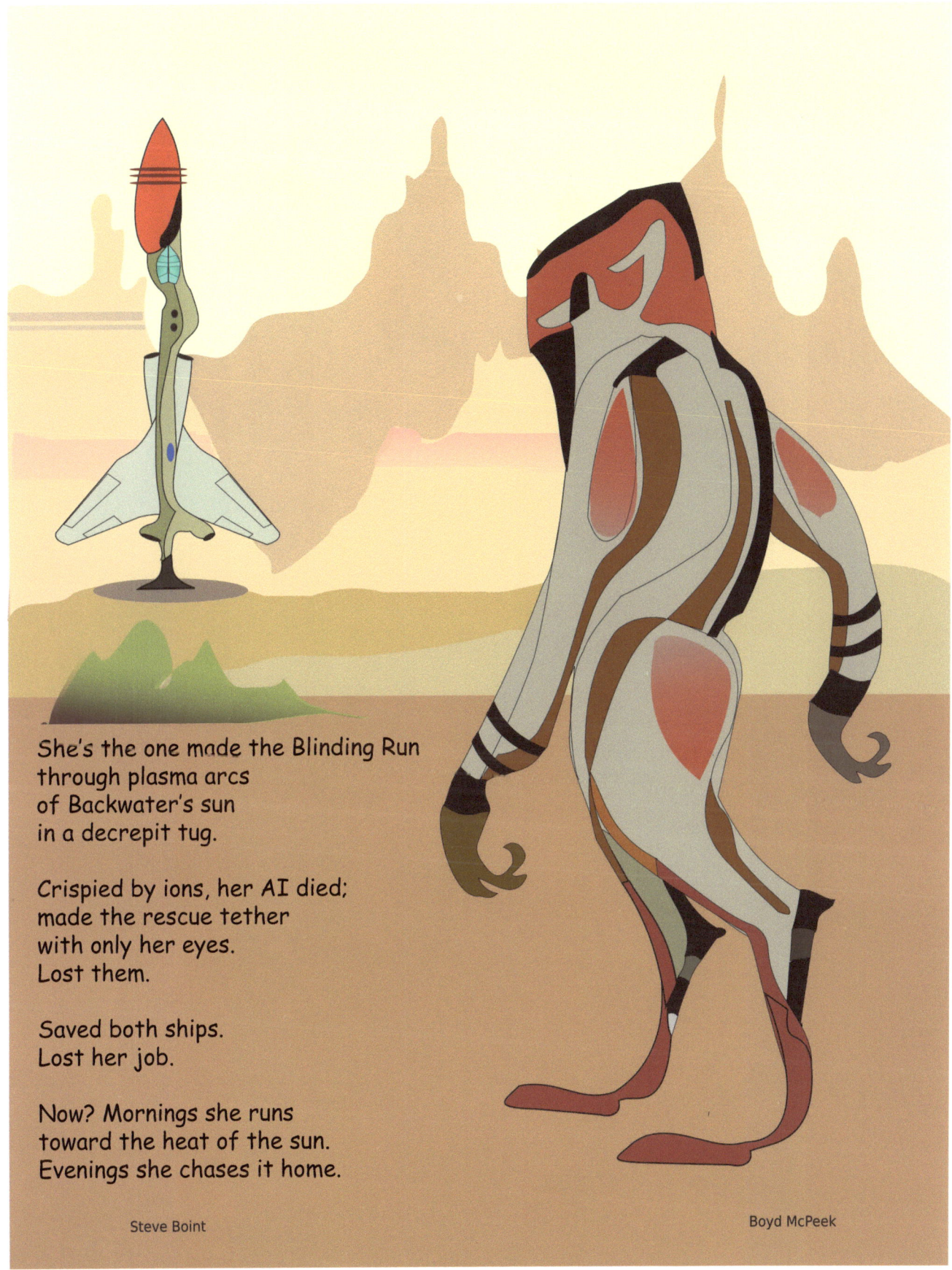

She's the one made the Blinding Run
through plasma arcs
of Backwater's sun
in a decrepit tug.

Crispied by ions, her AI died;
made the rescue tether
with only her eyes.
Lost them.

Saved both ships.
Lost her job.

Now? Mornings she runs
toward the heat of the sun.
Evenings she chases it home.

Steve Boint

Boyd McPeek

Learn

Should have known
a home must be grown.
Cobbled together,
it wobbles when weather
turns.

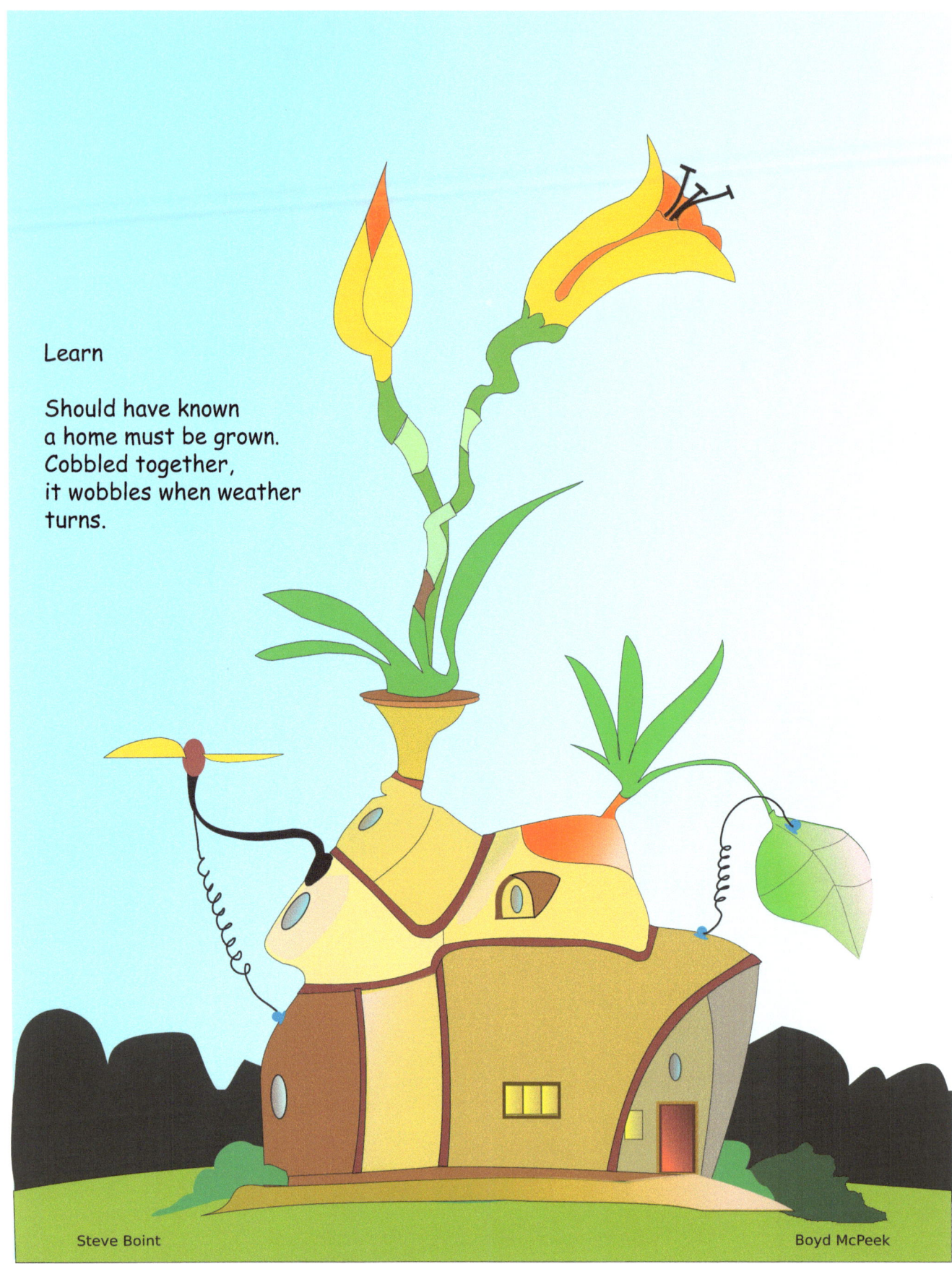

Steve Boint

Boyd McPeek

Transmission Home Upon Retirement

Gumdrop beetles backpedaling in the slough,
cabbage fish in season, and those shiny, tiny airlizards—
boil a net full to get the poison out and they taste good,
oxygen storms flapping the roof
like the whole place is high on life
keep my batteries charged,
no bosses,
no taxes—
couldn't have crashed in a better place.

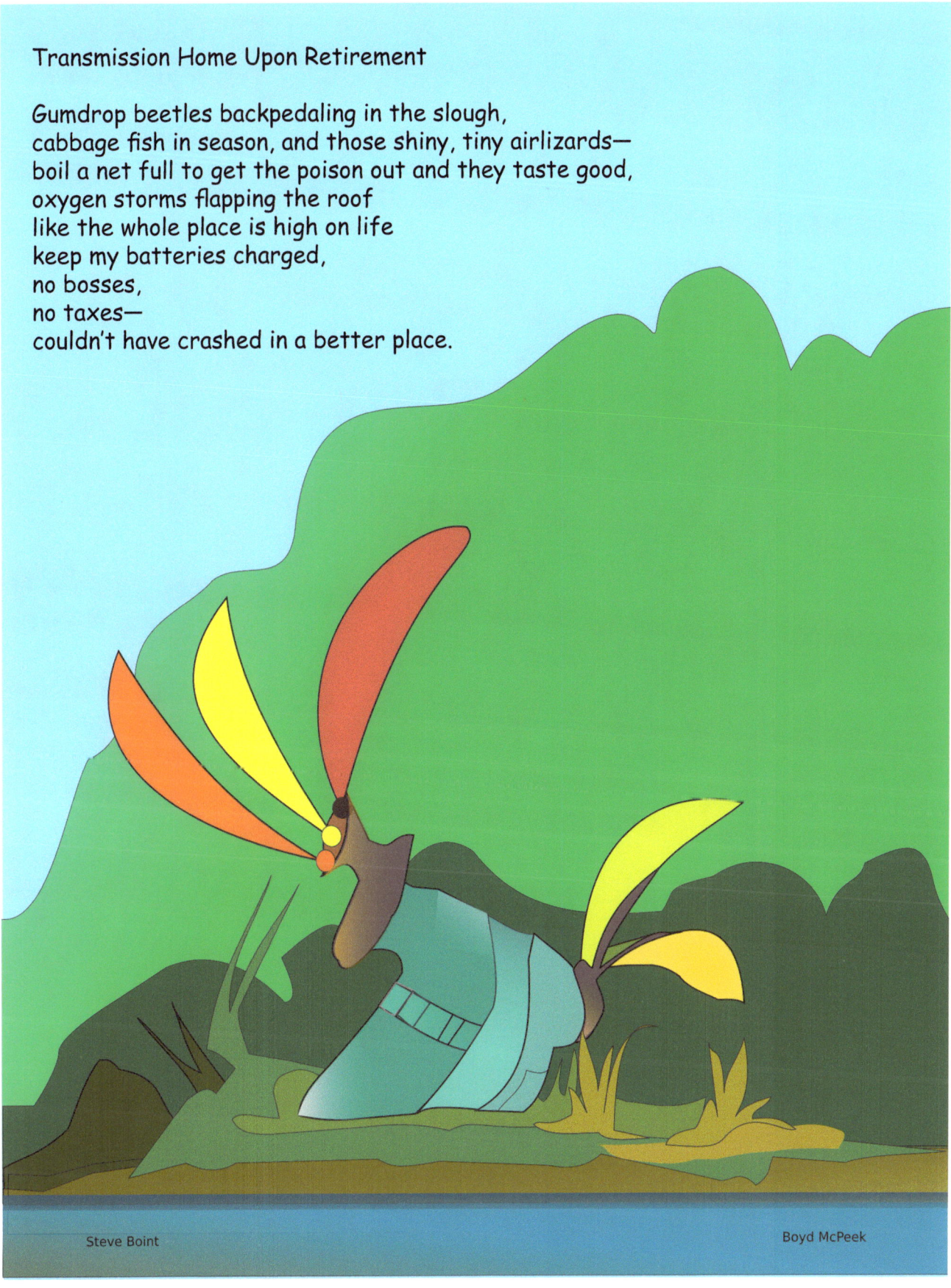

Steve Boint

Boyd McPeek

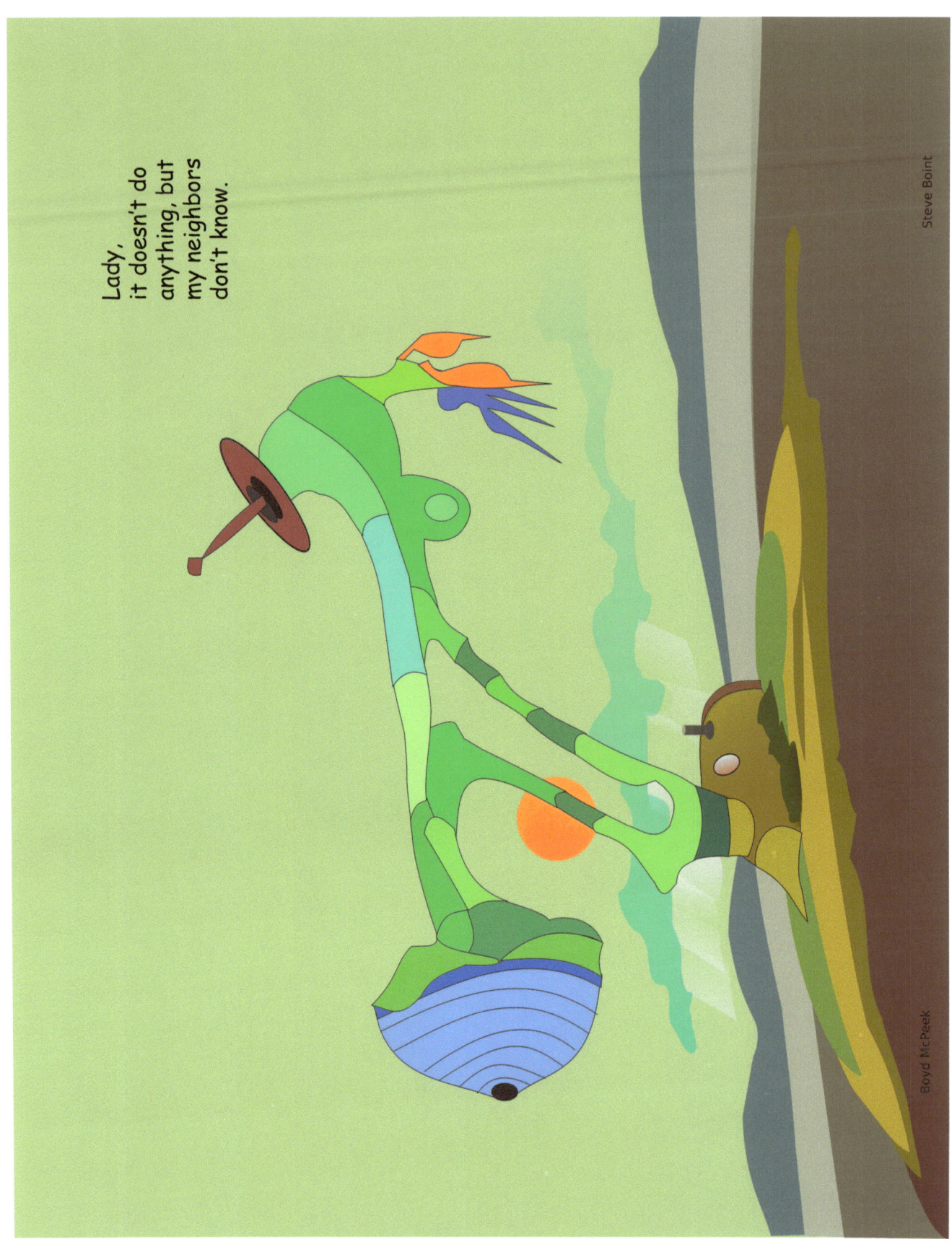

Lady,
it doesn't do
anything, but
my neighbors
don't know.

Boyd McPeek

Steve Boint

14

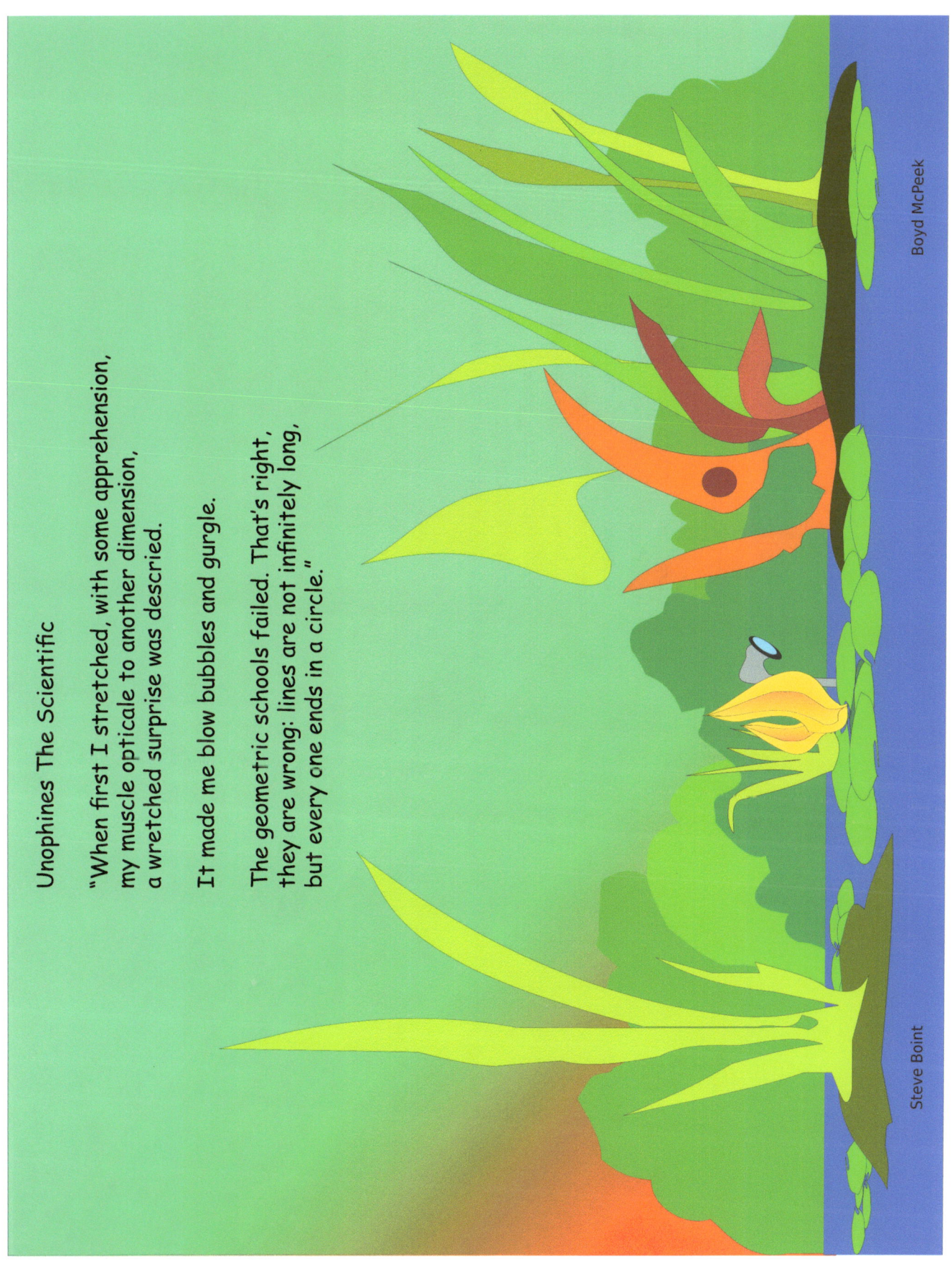

Unophines The Scientific

"When first I stretched, with some apprehension,
my muscle opticale to another dimension,
a wretched surprise was descried.

It made me blow bubbles and gurgle.

The geometric schools failed. That's right,
they are wrong: lines are not infinitely long,
but every one ends in a circle."

Boyd McPeek

Steve Boint

15

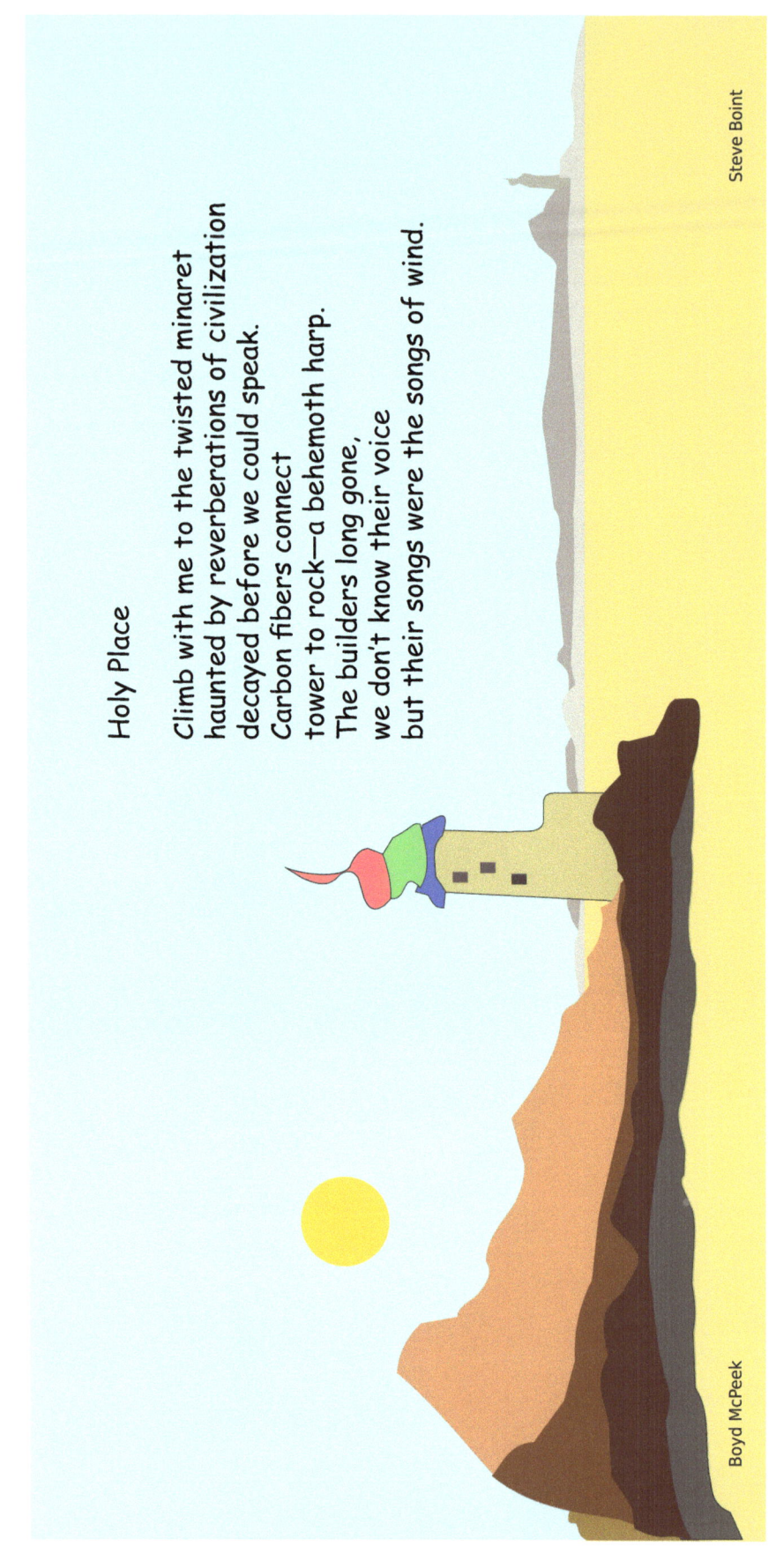

Holy Place

Climb with me to the twisted minaret
haunted by reverberations of civilization
decayed before we could speak.
Carbon fibers connect
tower to rock—a behemoth harp.
The builders long gone,
we don't know their voice
but their songs were the songs of wind.

Steve Boint

Boyd McPeek

16

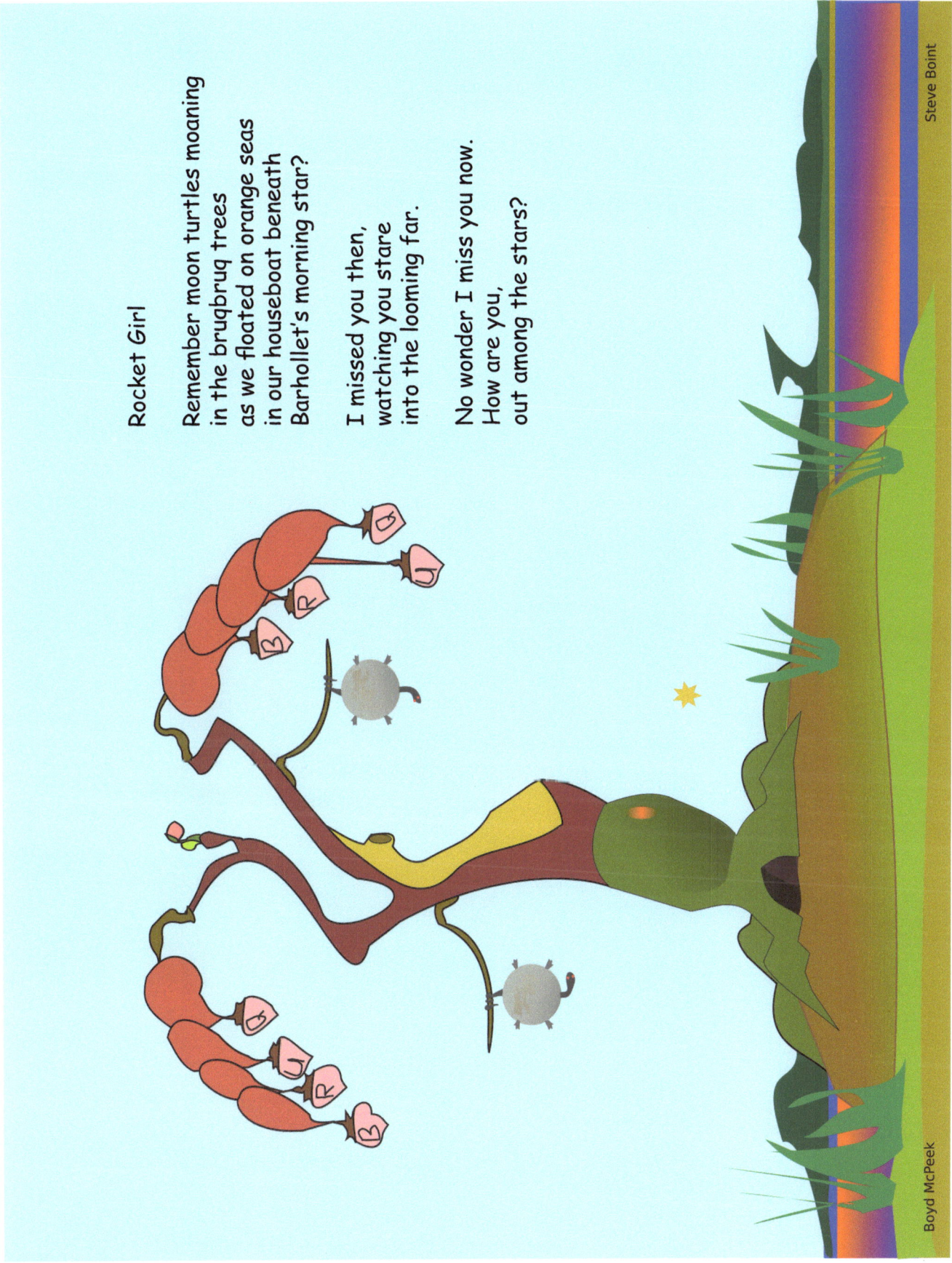

Rocket Girl

Remember moon turtles moaning
in the brugbruq trees
as we floated on orange seas
in our houseboat beneath
Barhollet's morning star?

I missed you then,
watching you stare
into the looming far.

No wonder I miss you now.
How are you,
out among the stars?

See
gasgrain slowly floating
as
through it we are boating.
Are you on the foredeck
noting sweet ammonia in the air?

Hear
rumbles in the distance
from
darkness far beneath us
as the thunderhead there
rushes, building upward through the air.

Feel
electrons dance upon
you.
The dream draws close around
you and the shadows chase
the cloudspray through your hair.

—A Lullaby Of The Cloud Gypsies

Steve Boint

Boyd McPeek

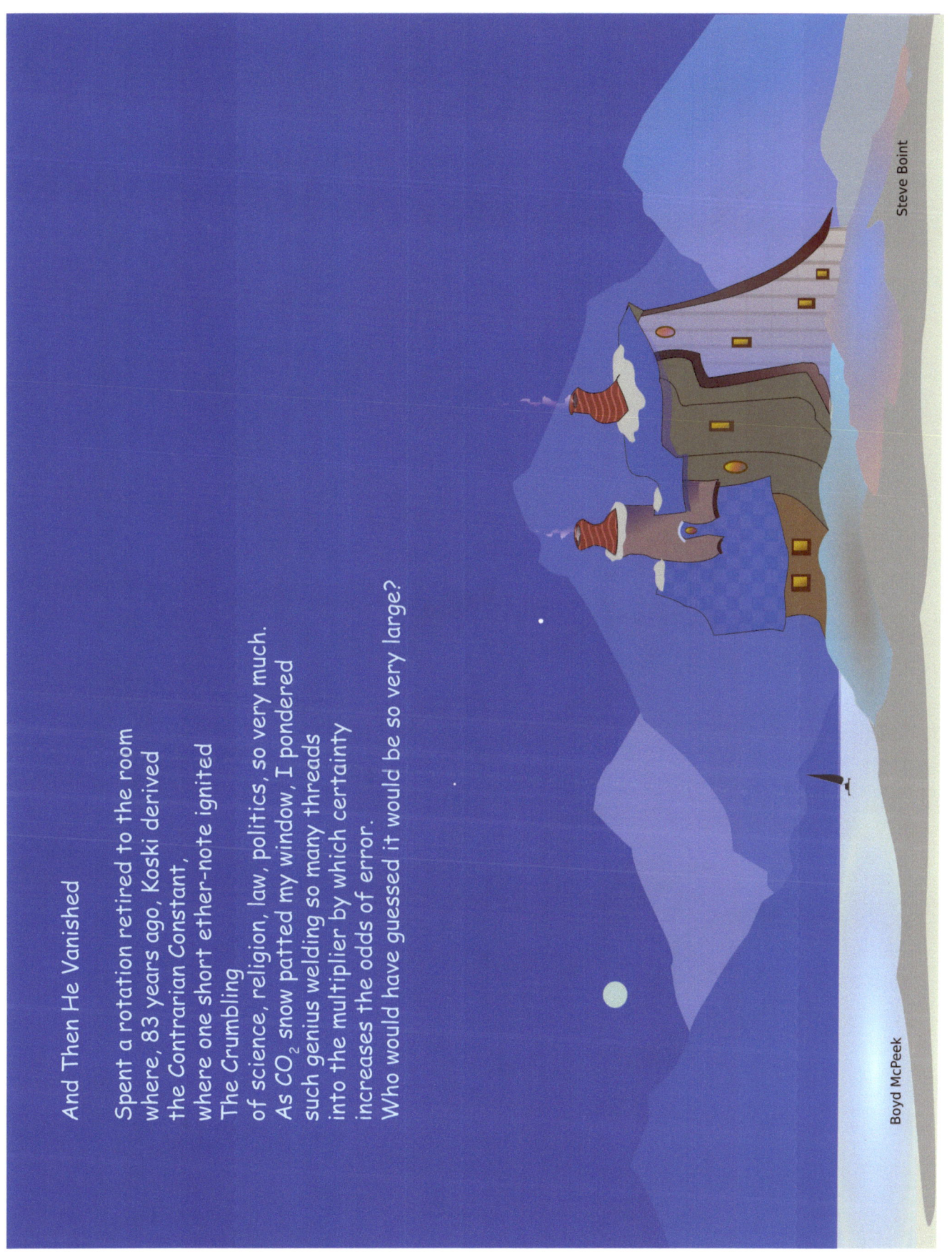

And Then He Vanished

Spent a rotation retired to the room
where, 83 years ago, Koski derived
the Contrarian Constant,
where one short ether-note ignited
The Crumbling
of science, religion, law, politics, so very much.
As CO_2 snow patted my window, I pondered
such genius welding so many threads
into the multiplier by which certainty
increases the odds of error.
Who would have guessed it would be so very large?

Boyd McPeek

Steve Boint

19

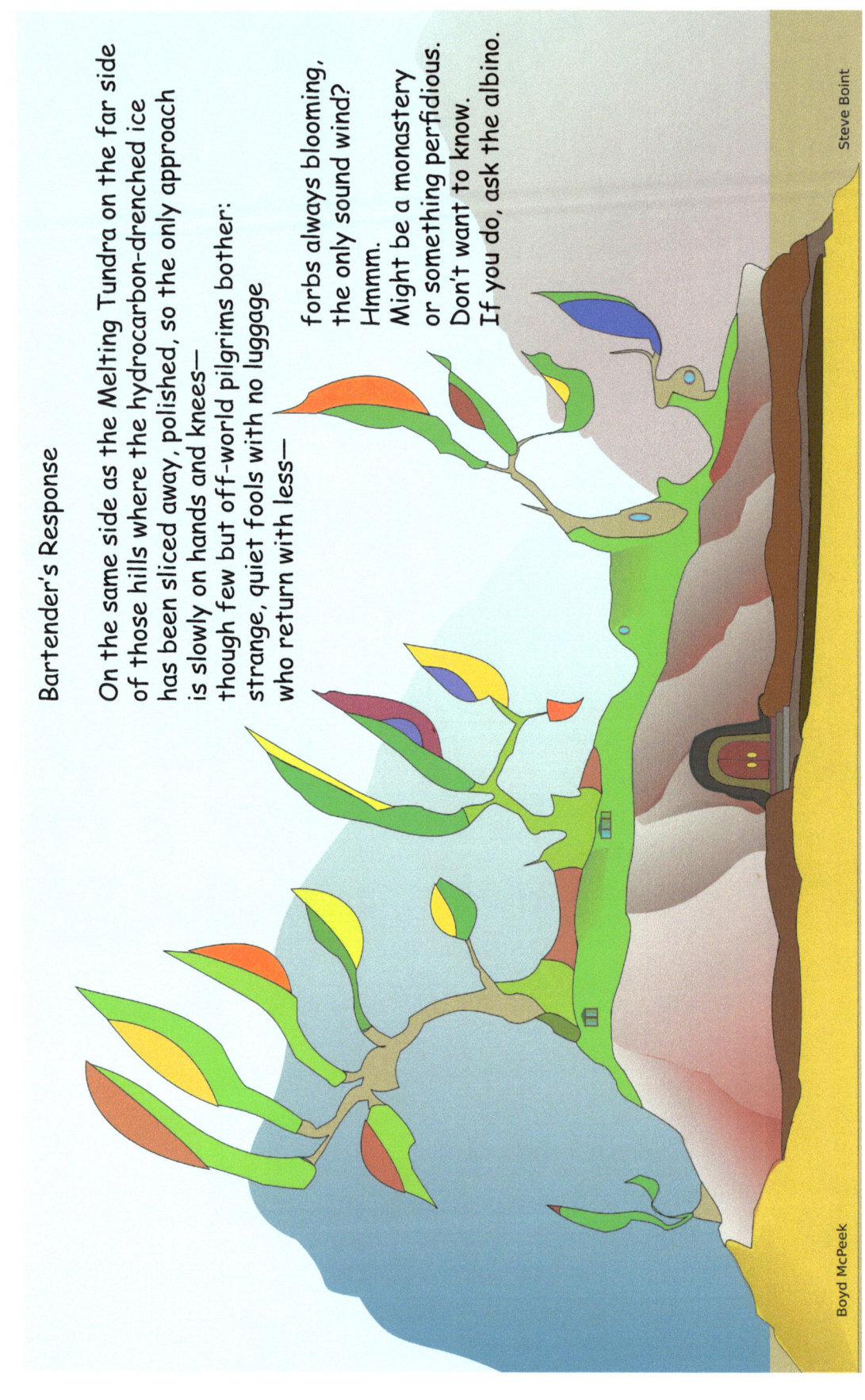

Bartender's Response

On the same side as the Melting Tundra on the far side
of those hills where the hydrocarbon-drenched ice
has been sliced away, polished, so the only approach
is slowly on hands and knees—
though few but off-world pilgrims bother:
strange, quiet fools with no luggage
who return with less—

forbs always blooming,
the only sound wind?
Hmmm.
Might be a monastery
or something perfidious.
Don't want to know.
If you do, ask the albino.

Boyd McPeek

Steve Boint

20

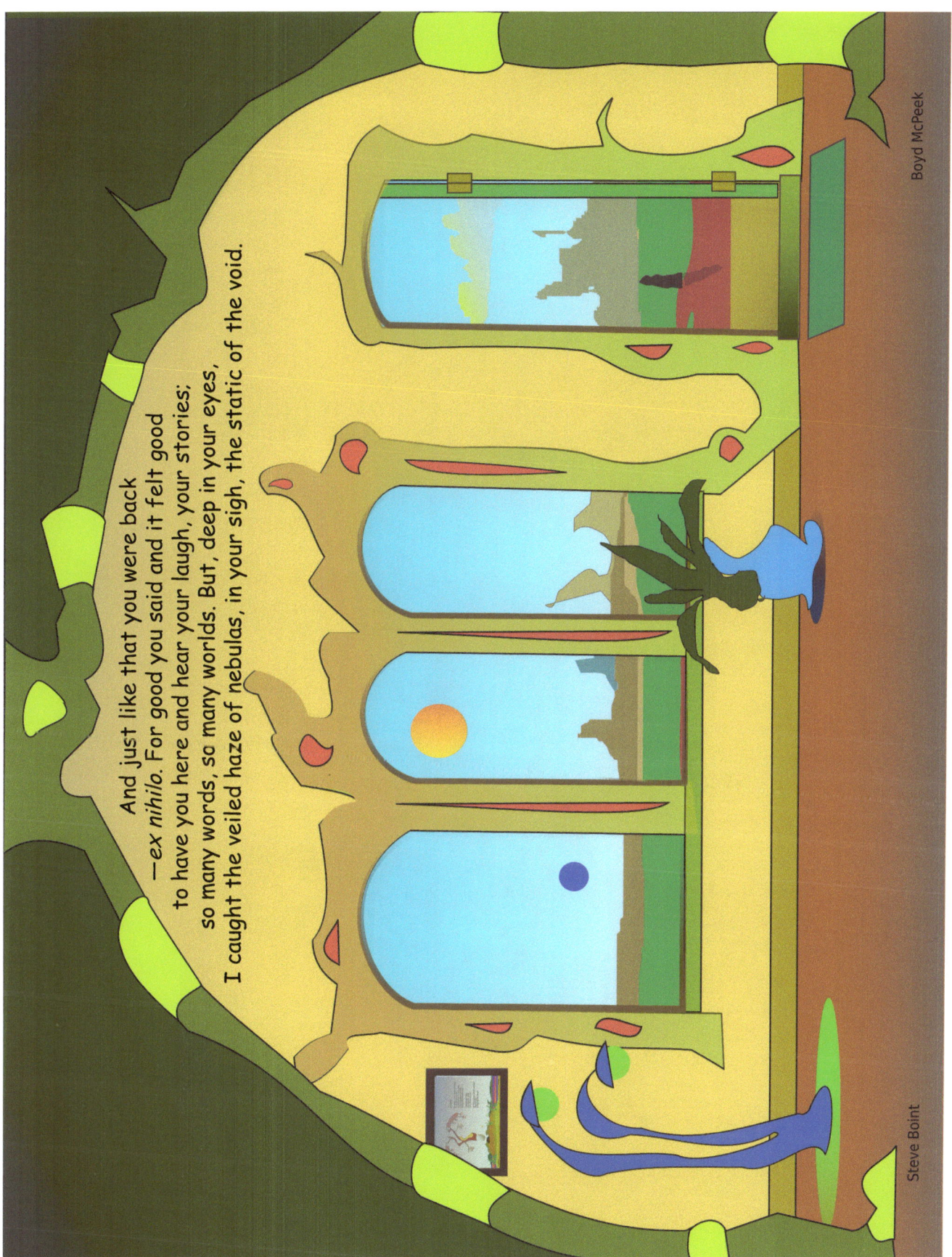

And just like that you were back
—*ex nihilo*. For good you said and it felt good
to have you here and hear your laugh, your stories;
so many words, so many worlds. But, deep in your eyes,
I caught the veiled haze of nebulas, in your sigh, the static of the void.

Boyd McPeek

Steve Boint

21

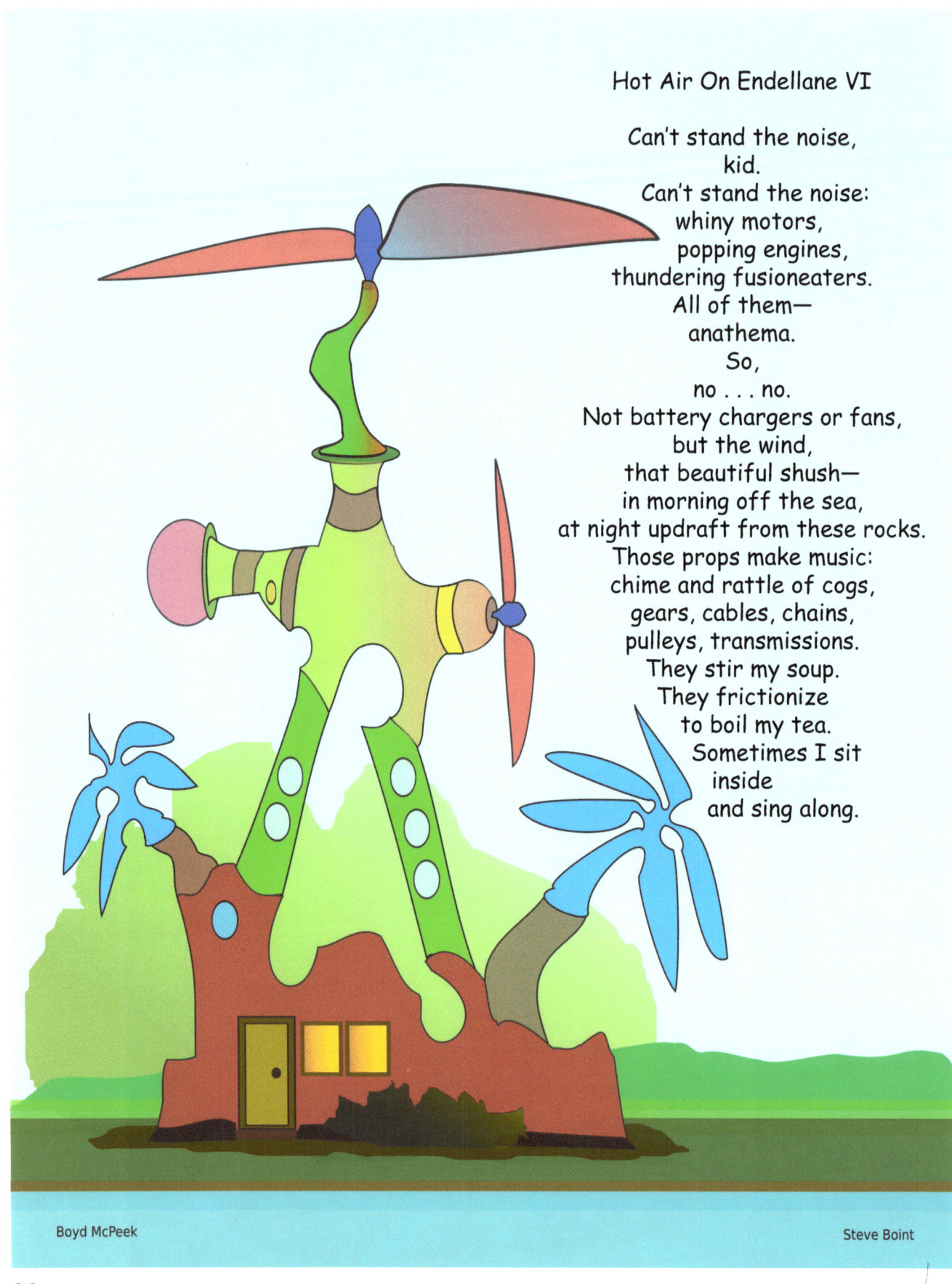

Hot Air On Endellane VI

Can't stand the noise,
    kid.
Can't stand the noise:
    whiny motors,
    popping engines,
thundering fusioneaters.
All of them—
    anathema.
    So,
    no . . . no.
Not battery chargers or fans,
    but the wind,
    that beautiful shush—
in morning off the sea,
at night updraft from these rocks.
    Those props make music:
    chime and rattle of cogs,
    gears, cables, chains,
    pulleys, transmissions.
    They stir my soup.
    They frictionize
        to boil my tea.
        Sometimes I sit
        inside
        and sing along.

Boyd McPeek

Steve Boint

22

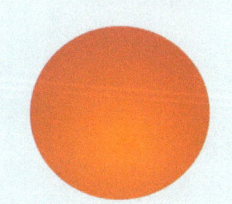

Lost a spitting match
in the deserts of Dviin
to a foul-mouthed grumpel.

I let him win.

Poor cuss:
life had humped him
a few too many times.

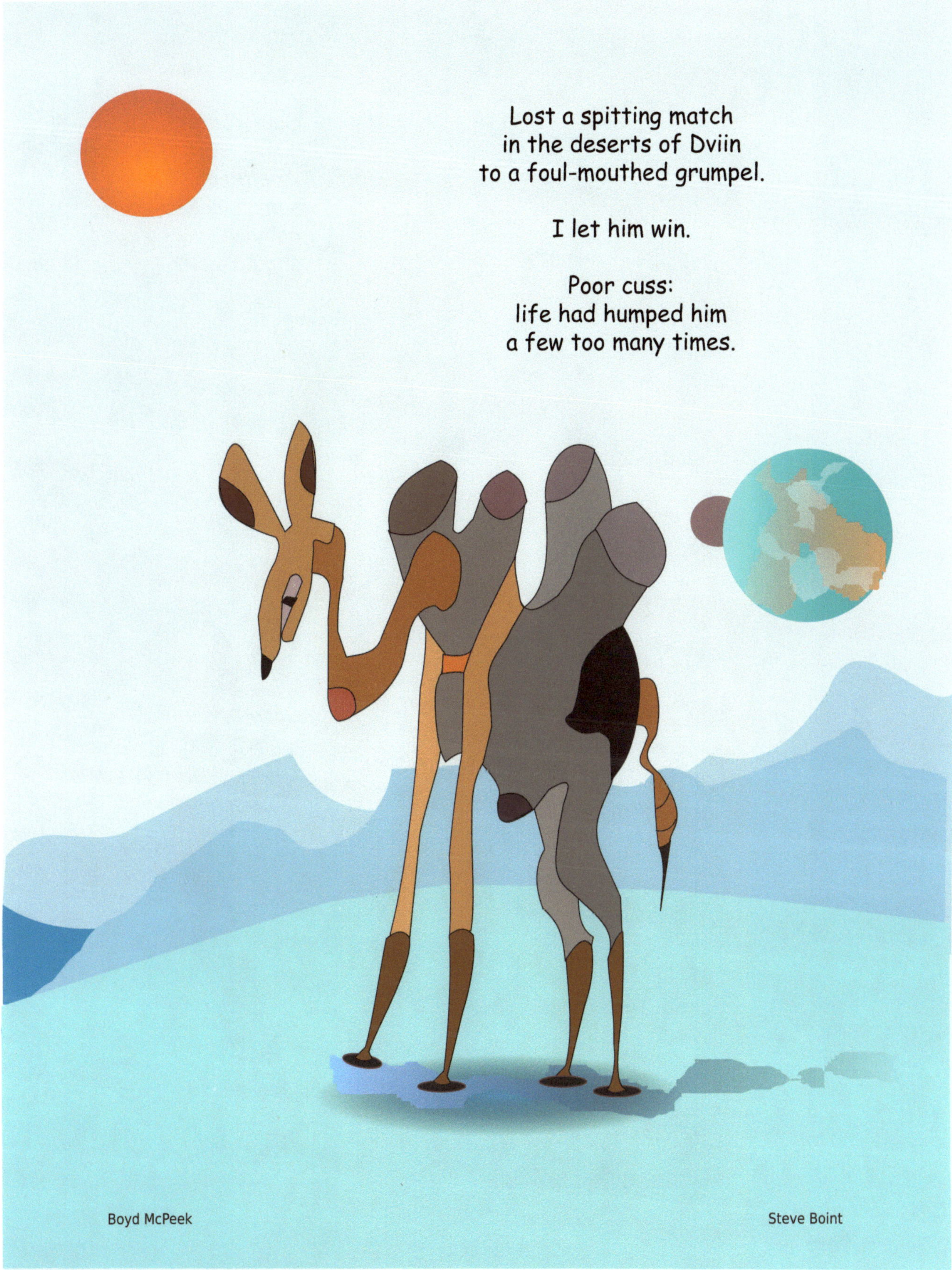

Boyd McPeek   Steve Boint

23

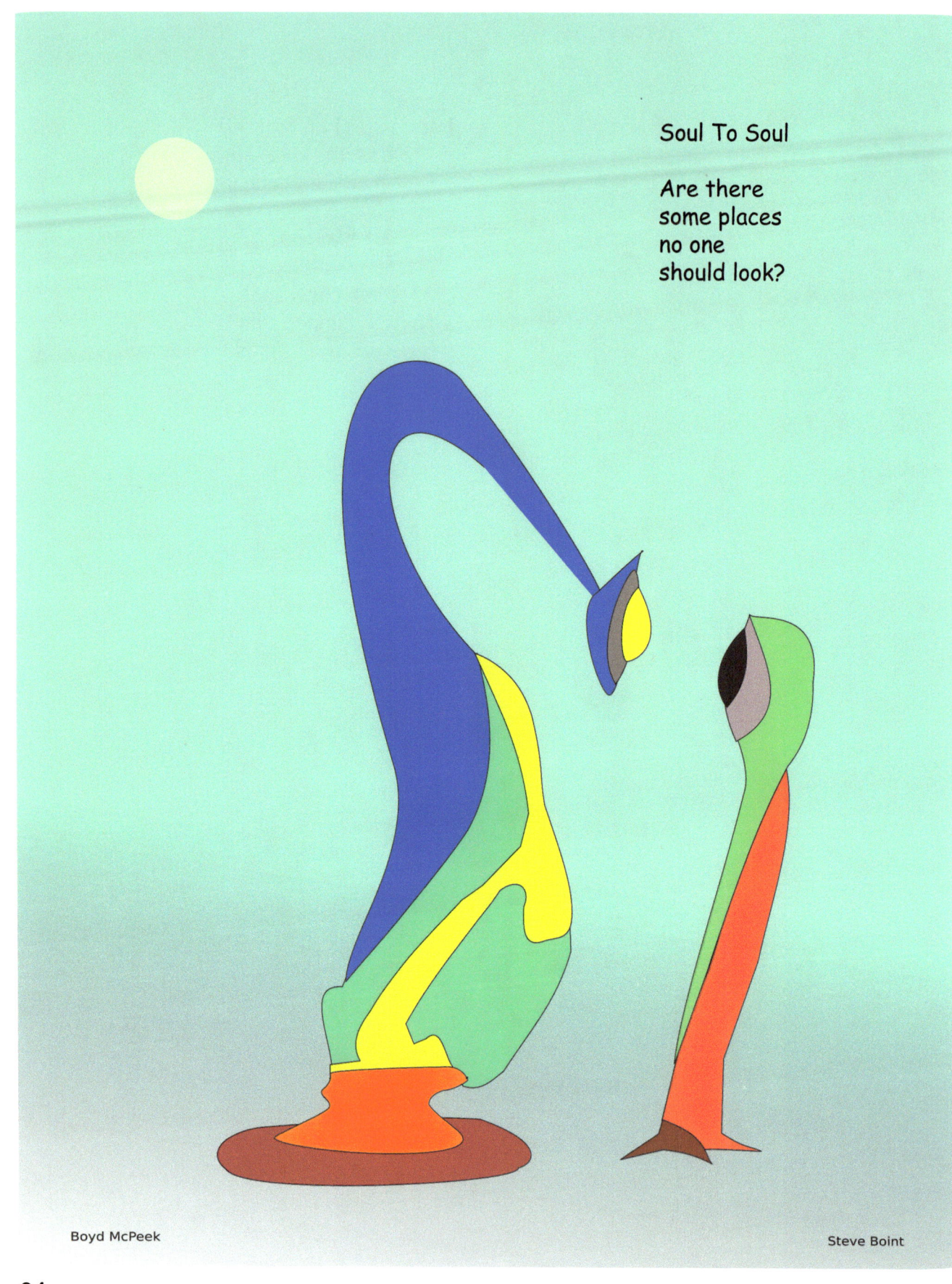

Soul To Soul

Are there
some places
no one
should look?

Boyd McPeek

Steve Boint

24

Before the argon winds of the fifth month,
late, as the salmongar run begins
to abate, near a beach
where septopods sleep,
there's a cabin for rent:
a bargain, not to be missed—
days spent sleeping,
at night we'd fish.

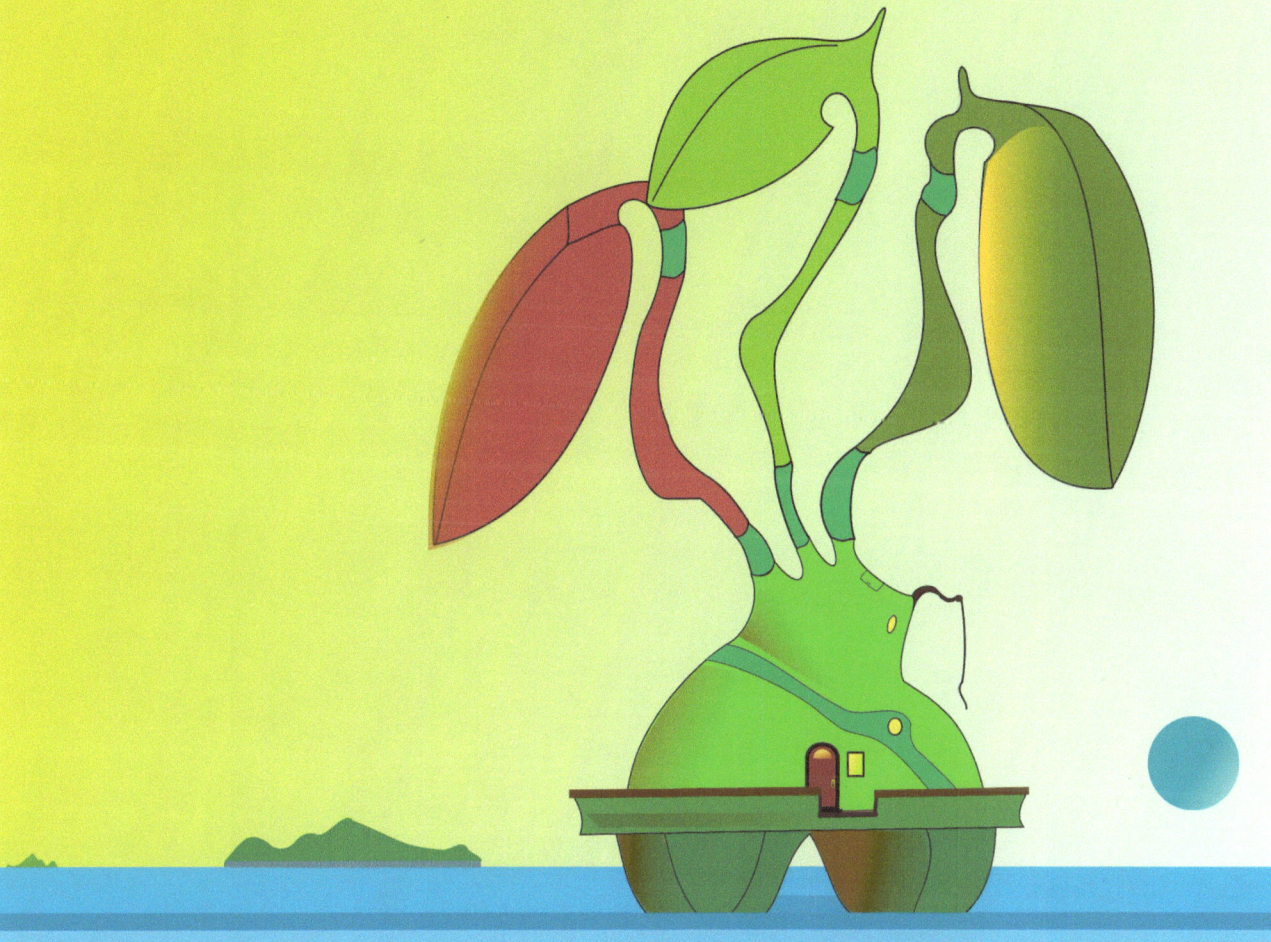

Steve Boint

Boyd McPeek

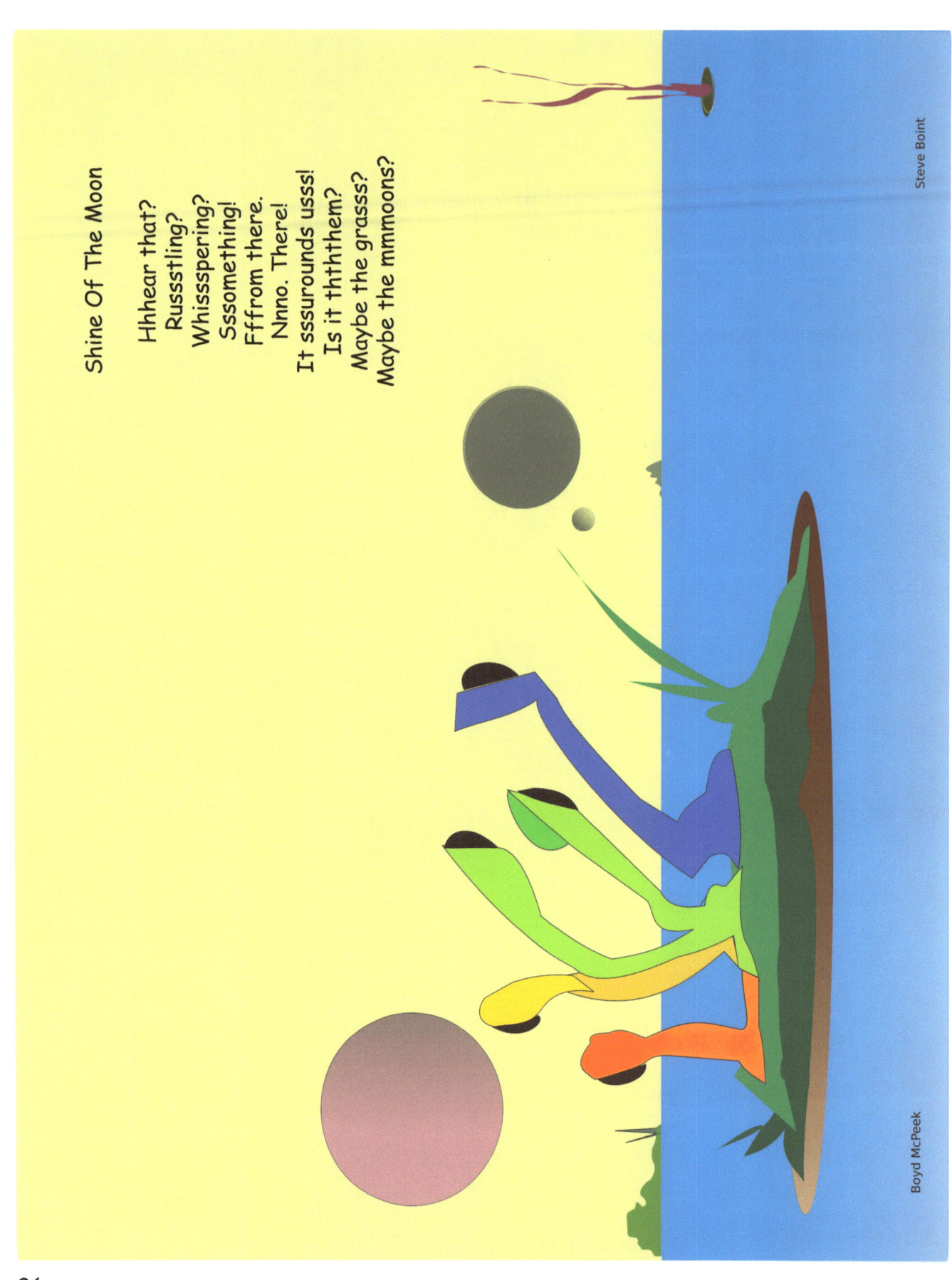

Shine Of The Moon

Hhhear that?
Russstling?
Whissspering?
Sssomething!
Fffrom there.
Nnno. There!
It sssurounds usss!
Is it thththem?
Maybe the grasss?
Maybe the mmmoons?

Boyd McPeek

Steve Boint

26

Empirical Method

Like I told you: shovel deep
enough and find tonight.
Must flow underneath. Now,
fill it so it doesn't leak.
We'll go back this evening
and dig for light.

Steve Boint

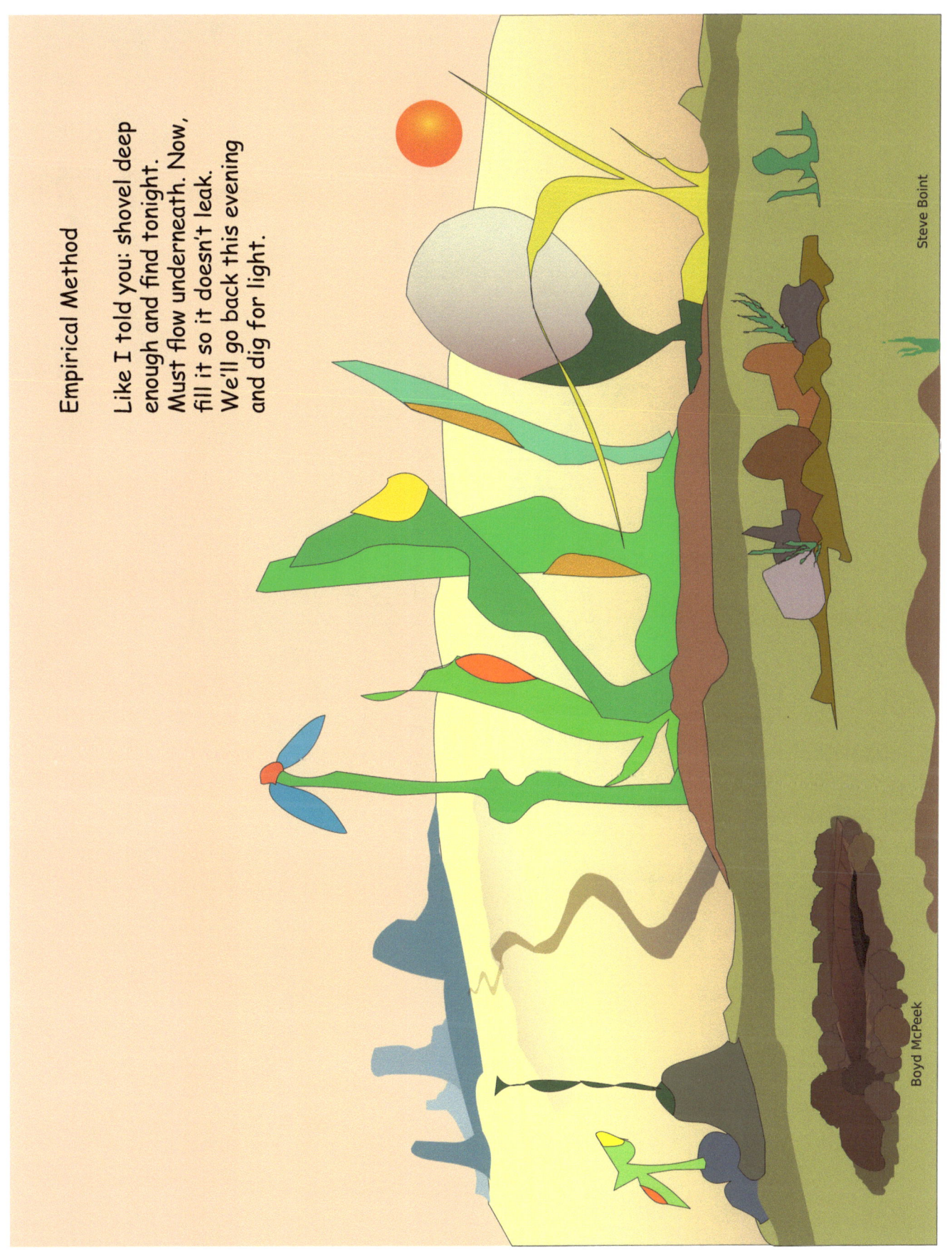

Boyd McPeek

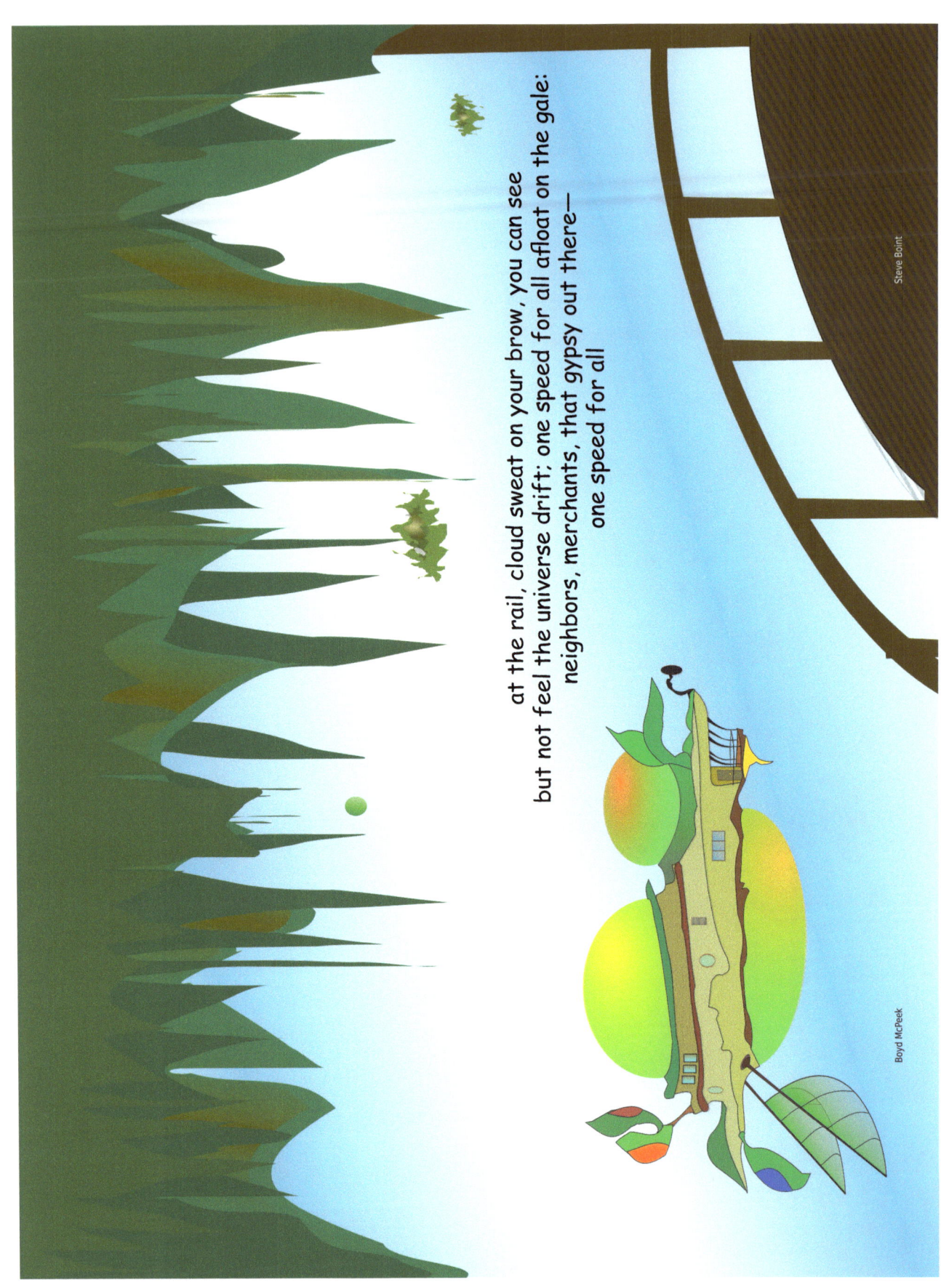

at the rail, cloud sweat on your brow, you can see
but not feel the universe drift; one speed for all afloat on the gale:
neighbors, merchants, that gypsy out there—
one speed for all

Steve Boint

Boyd McPeek

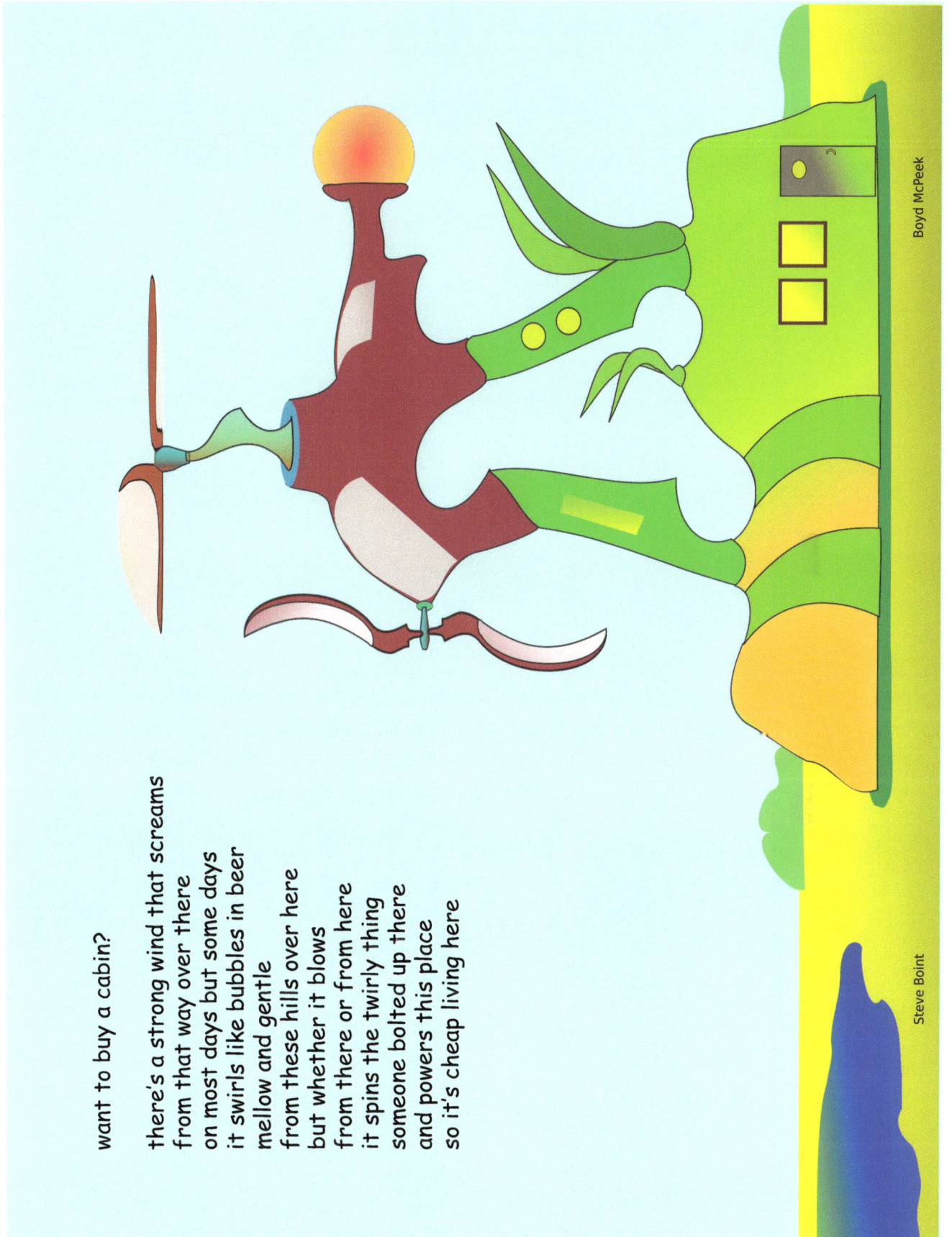

want to buy a cabin?

there's a strong wind that screams
from that way over there
on most days but some days
it swirls like bubbles in beer
mellow and gentle
from these hills over here
but whether it blows
from there or from here
it spins the twirly thing
someone bolted up there
and powers this place
so it's cheap living here

Boyd McPeek

Steve Boint

but this one, not the others, only this one whispered to me.

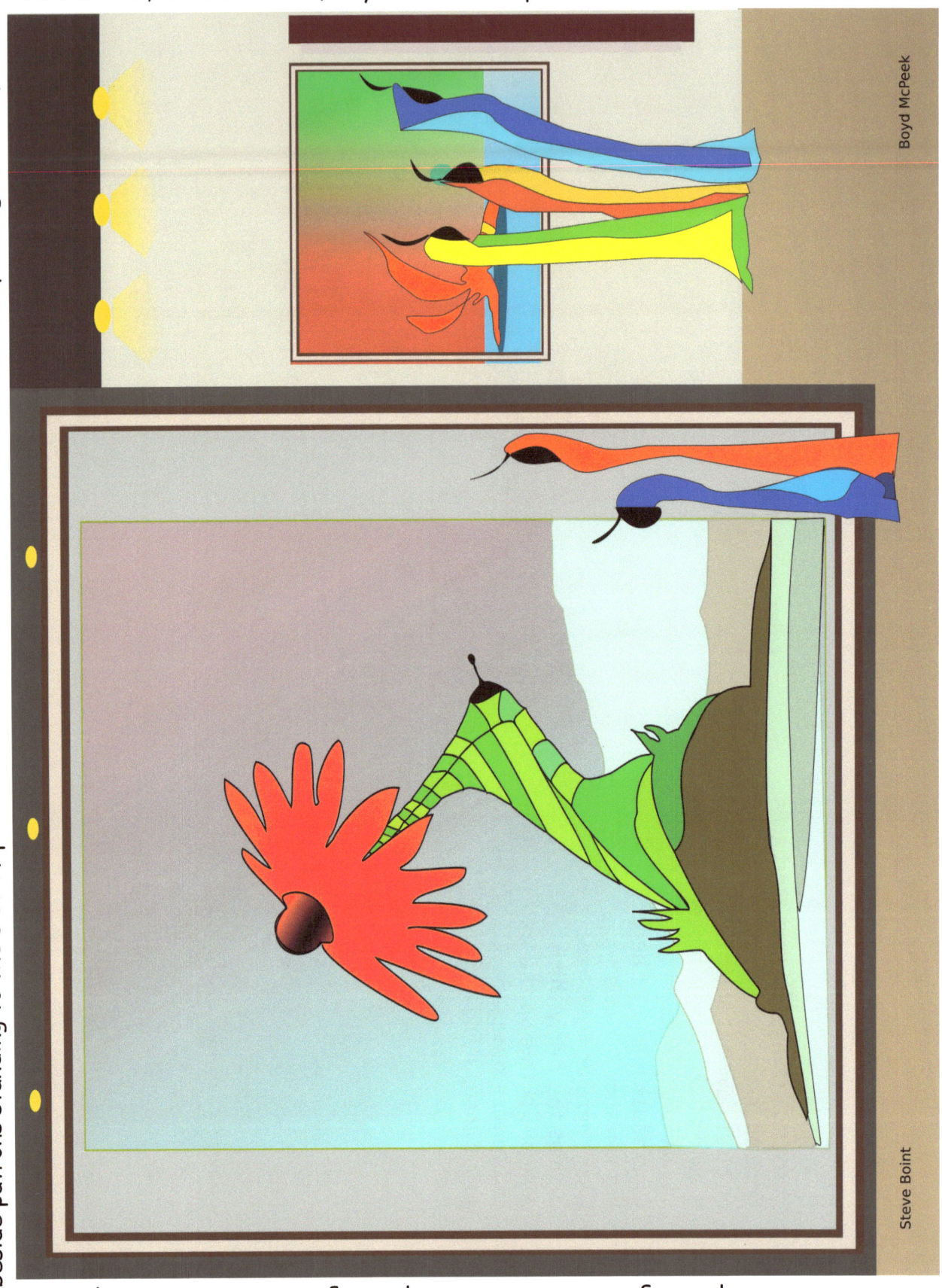

Boyd McPeek

Steve Boint

beside patrons standing to the side of patrons was a flower like the flowers on the other paintings before patrons,

On a painting on the wall beside a painting on a wall in front of patrons

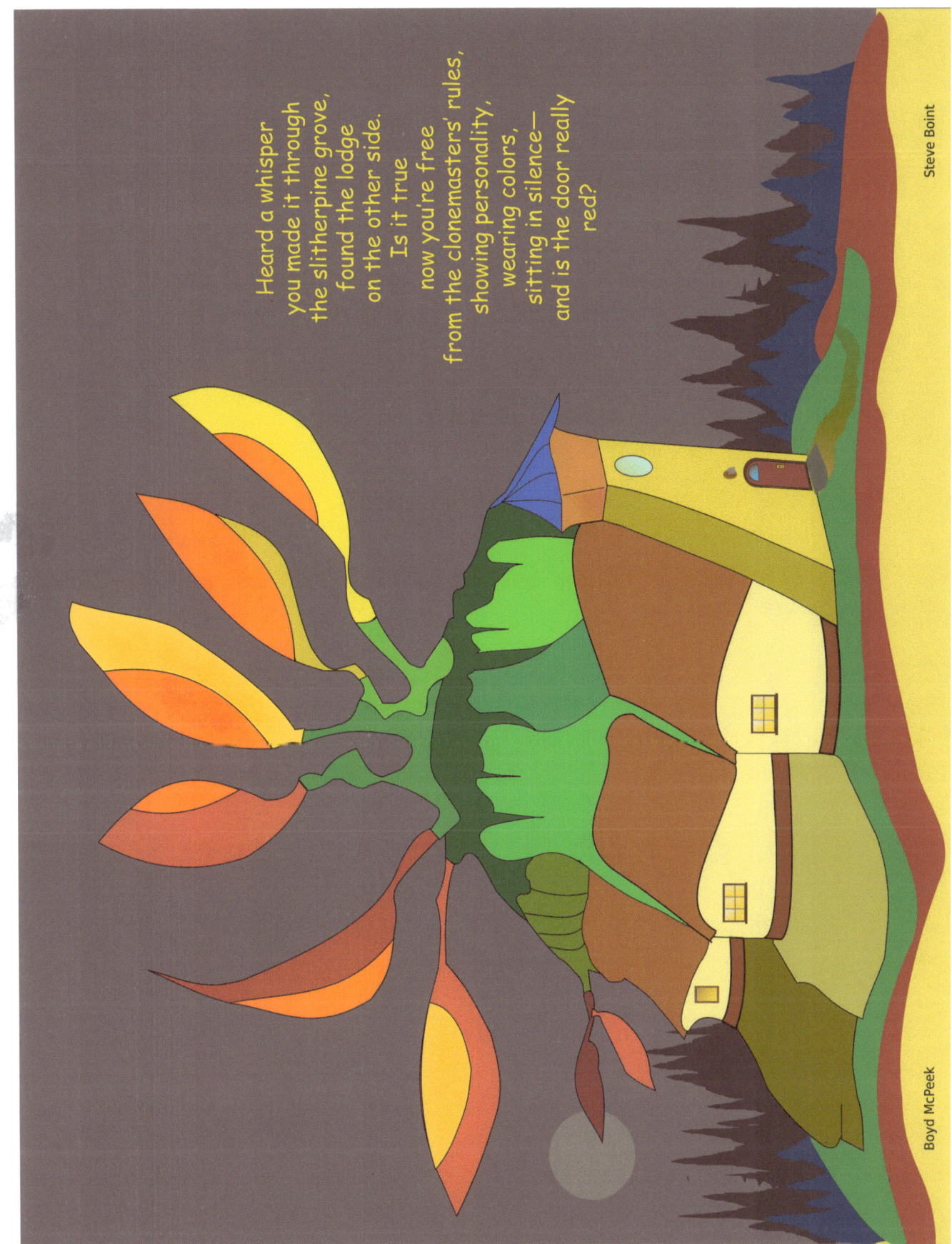

Heard a whisper
you made it through
the slitherpine grove,
found the lodge
on the other side.
Is it true
now you're free
from the clonemasters' rules,
showing personality,
wearing colors,
sitting in silence—
and is the door really
red?

Steve Boint

Boyd McPeek

31

Translucence

Zamboni driver, me,
for the sail-razor races on the Bombglass Sea.

Then—
groan of massive ships balanced on blades slicing down the grooves their keels made.
Days of polishing a city turned to glass in some war sometime between unknowns.
Gaze down through smoky swirls and clouds, through amber, fuchsia, brown, and time,
and, if the light was right, the buffing fine, see forms of cities and perhaps them.

Last week—
collecting overtime beneath the tri-moons' light,
best shine ever, got it just right.
Glanced down, saw deeper than before.

Zamboni driver, me,
booking passage through the deep;
travel far, travel long,
find someplace I can sleep.

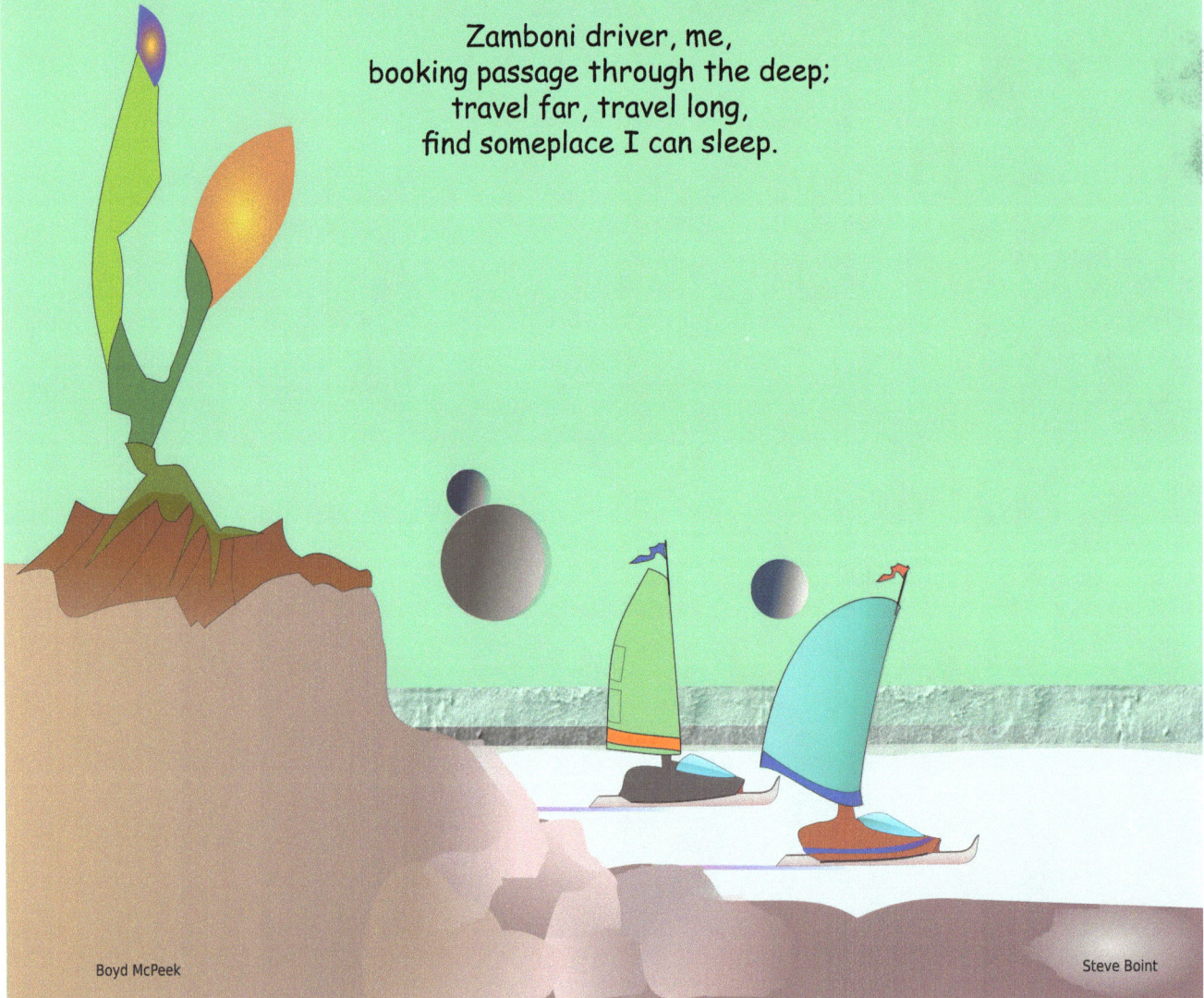

Boyd McPeek

Steve Boint

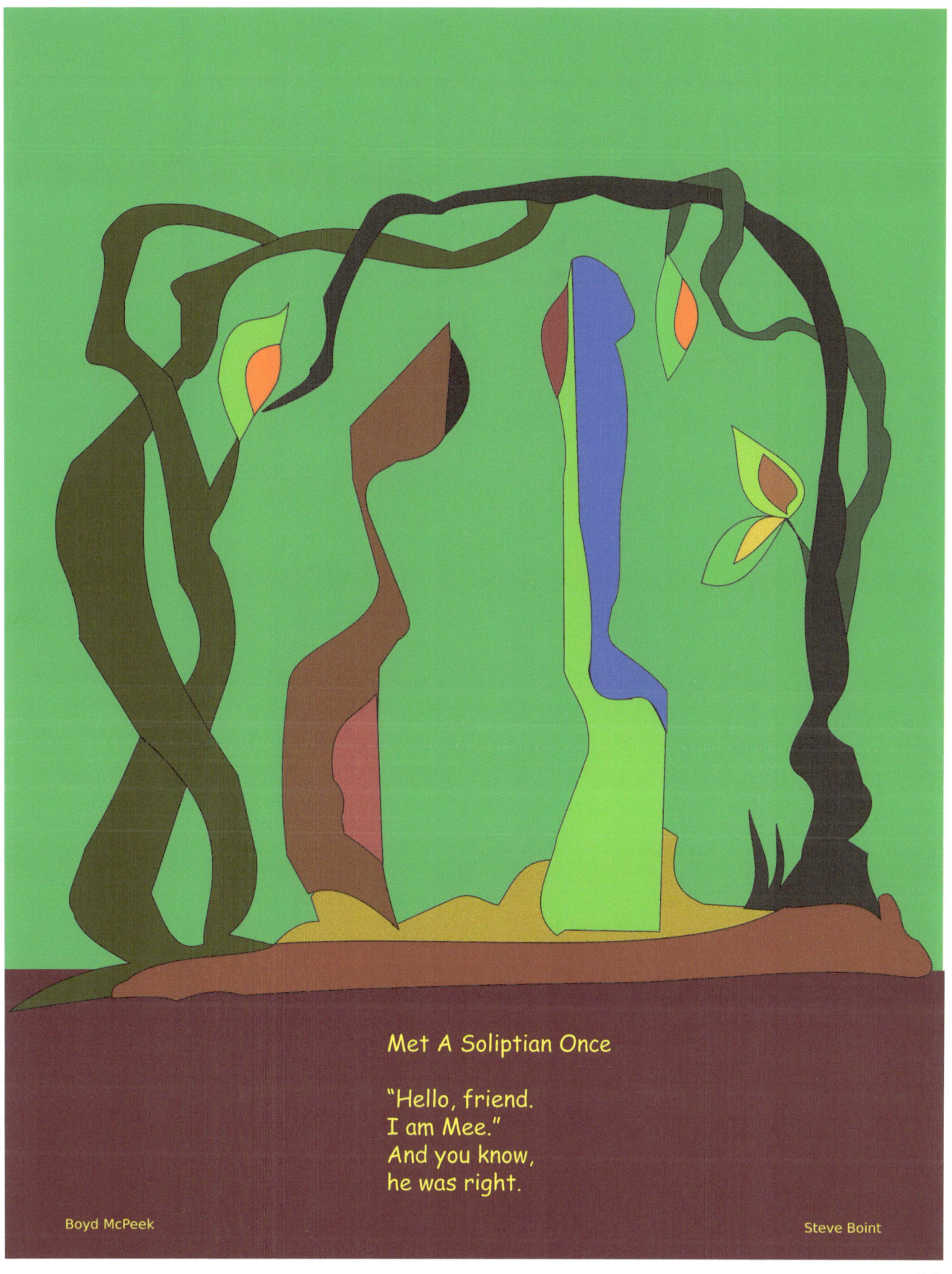

Met A Soliptian Once

"Hello, friend.
I am Mee."
And you know,
he was right.

Boyd McPeek

Steve Boint

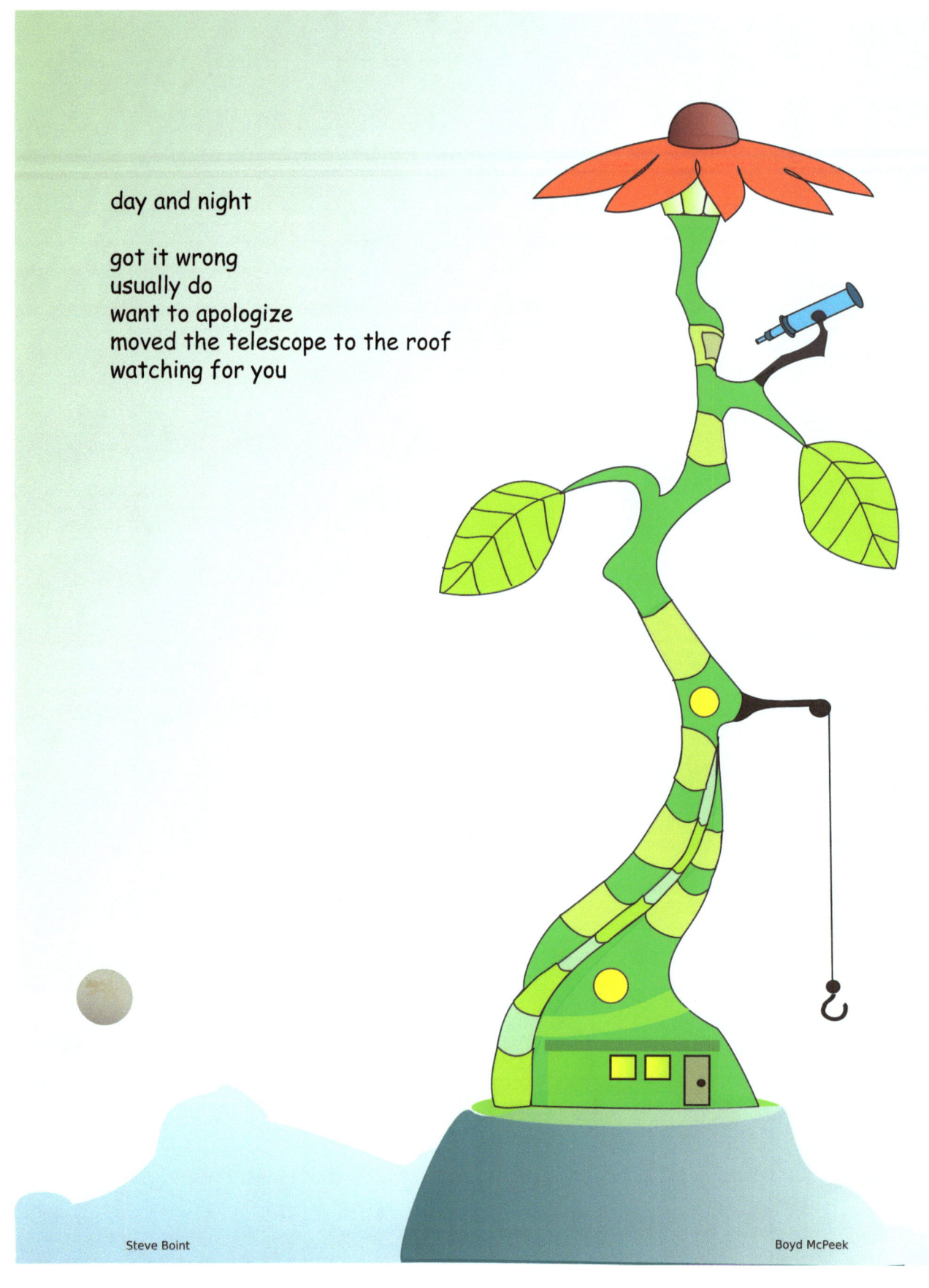

day and night

got it wrong
usually do
want to apologize
moved the telescope to the roof
watching for you

Steve Boint

Boyd McPeek

34

On the cusp of Creghorn Crevasse
where undergrowth grows over
what passes for a road,
an ancient house crouches
on overgrowth grown under
its foundation.
At the spaceport, you can find
hundred-year-old holos
from when humans
first arrived, bits of early
robo surveys have survived.
That shed
is already there.
Looks the same.
For all I know,
its door still opens.
Never tried it.
Never will.

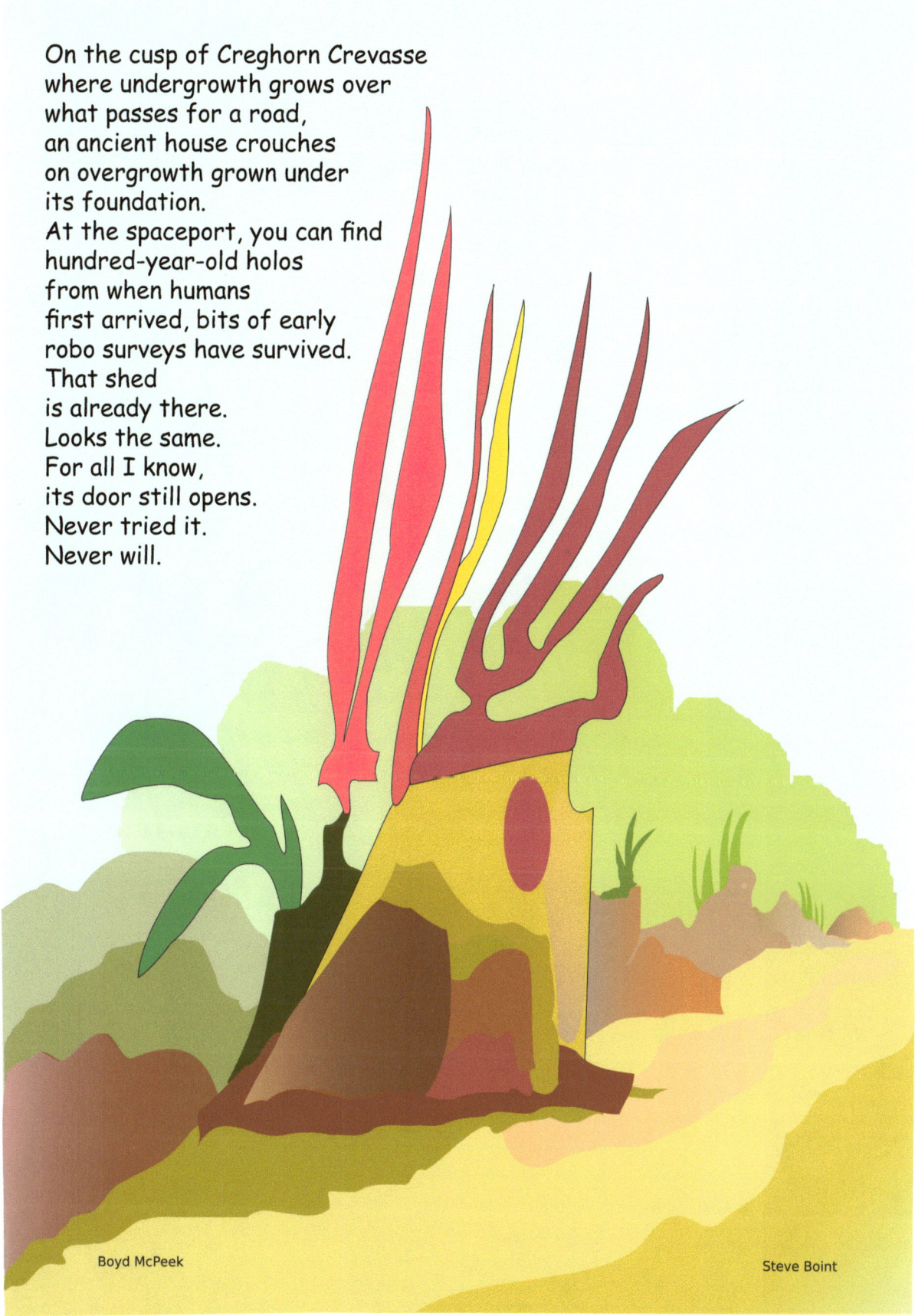

Boyd McPeek

Steve Boint

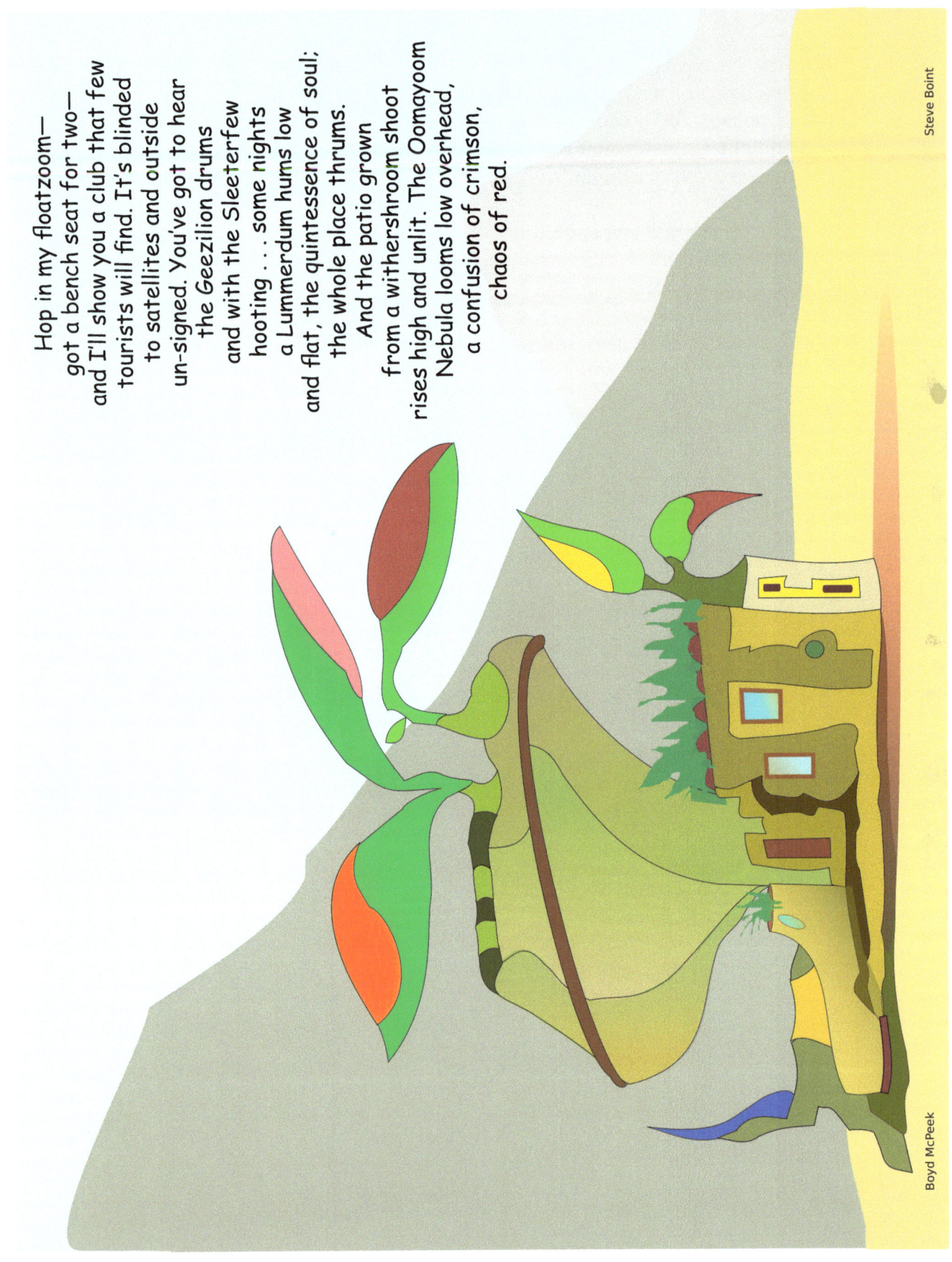

Hop in my floatzoom—
got a bench seat for two—
and I'll show you a club that few
tourists will find. It's blinded
to satellites and outside
un-signed. You've got to hear
the *Geezilion* drums
and with the *Sleeterfew*
hooting . . . some nights
a *Lummerdum* hums low
and flat, the quintessence of soul:
the whole place thrums.
And the patio grown
from a withershroom shoot
rises high and unlit. The *Oomayoom*
Nebula looms low overhead,
a confusion of crimson,
chaos of red.

Steve Boint

Boyd McPeek

36

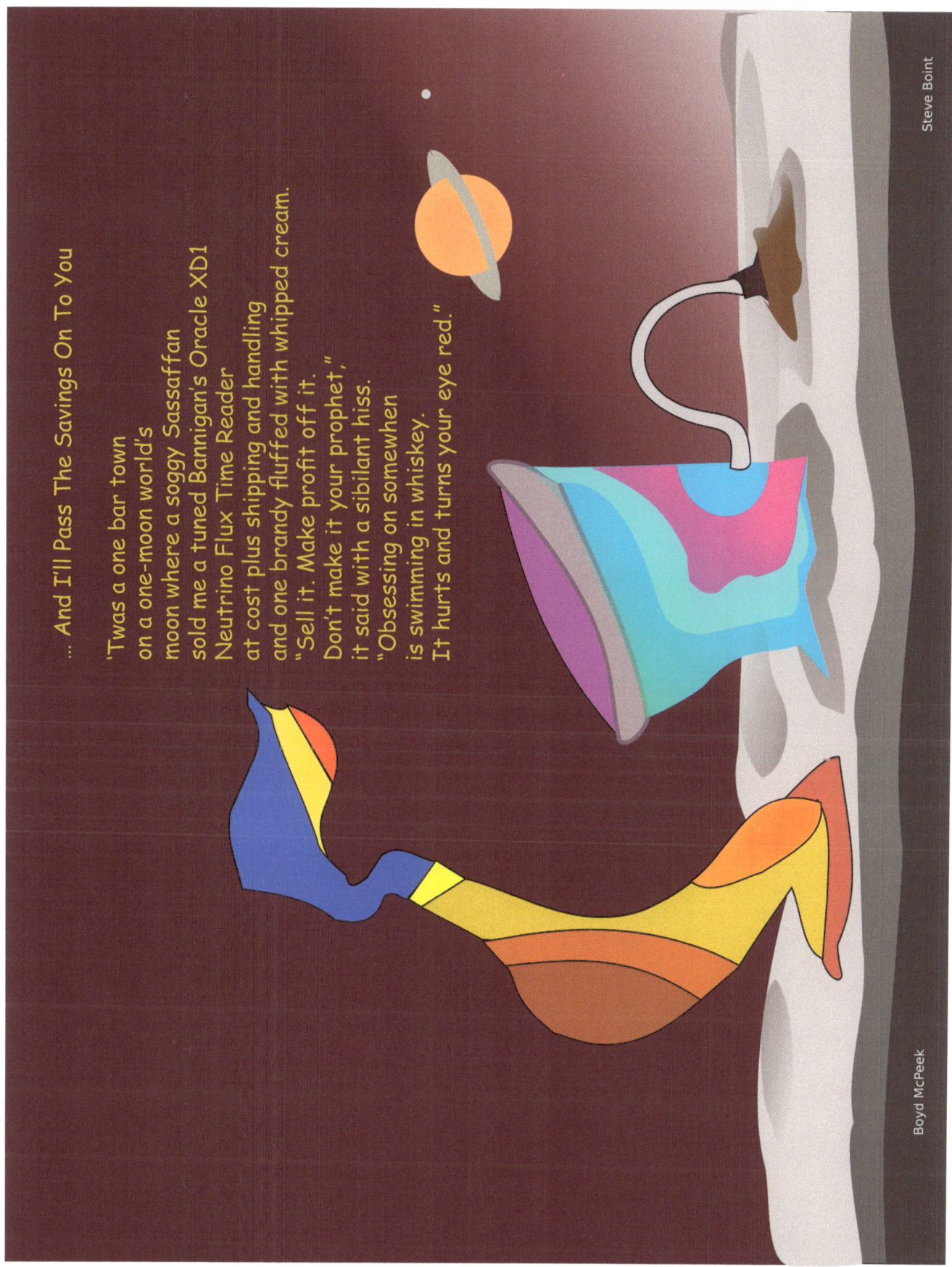

... And I'll Pass The Savings On To You

"Twas a one bar town
on a one-moon world's
moon where a soggy Sassaffan
sold me a tuned Bannigan's Oracle XD1
Neutrino Flux Time Reader
at cost plus shipping and handling
and one brandy fluffed with whipped cream.
"Sell it. Make profit off it.
Don't make it your prophet,"
it said with a sibilant hiss.
"Obsessing on somewhen
is swimming in whiskey.
It hurts and turns your eye red."

Steve Boint

Boyd McPeek

37

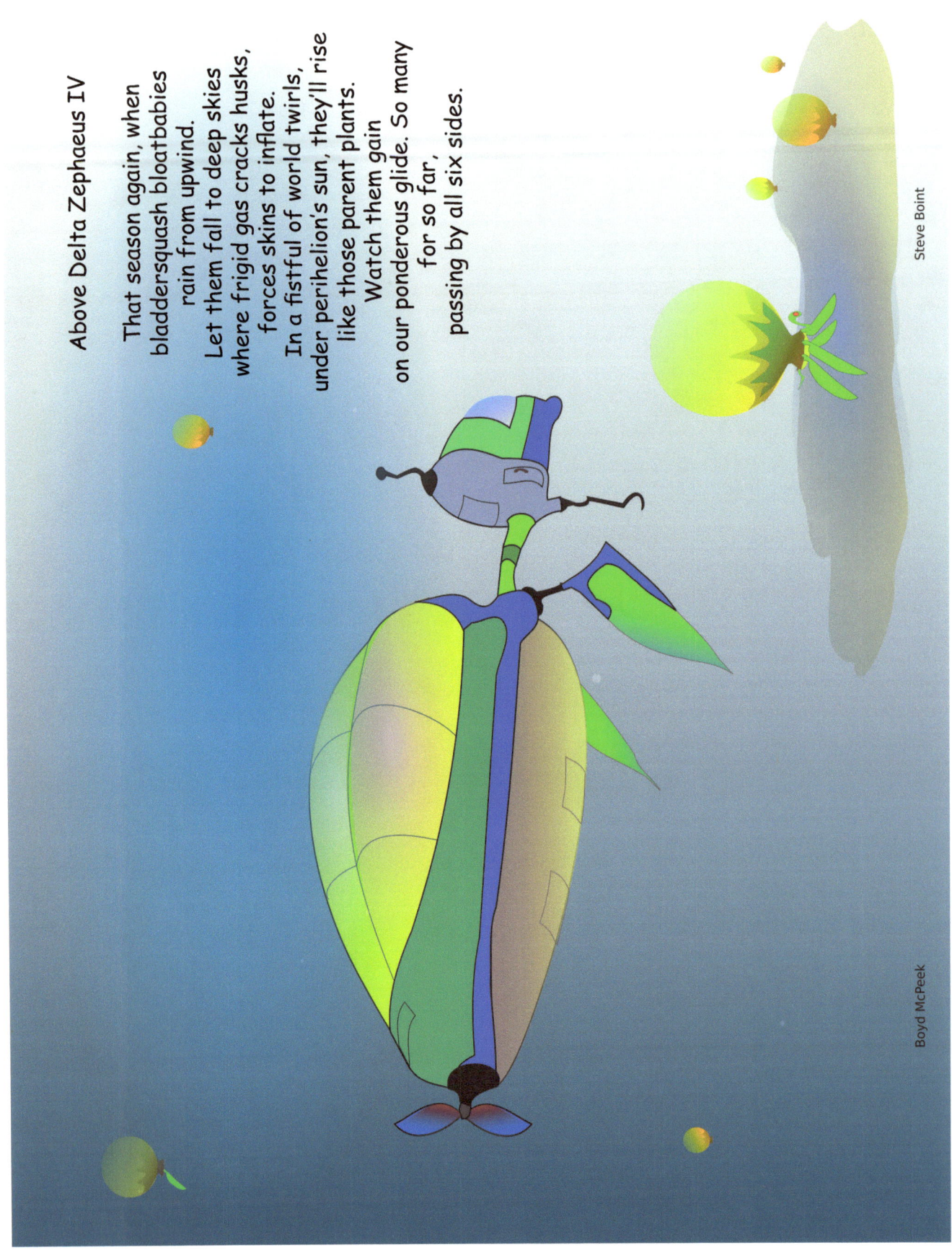

Above Delta Zephaeus IV

That season again, when
bladdersquash bloatbabies
rain from upwind.
Let them fall to deep skies
where frigid gas cracks husks,
forces skins to inflate.
In a fistful of world twirls,
under perihelion's sun, they'll rise
like those parent plants.
Watch them gain
on our ponderous glide. So many
for so far,
passing by all six sides.

Steve Boint

Boyd McPeek

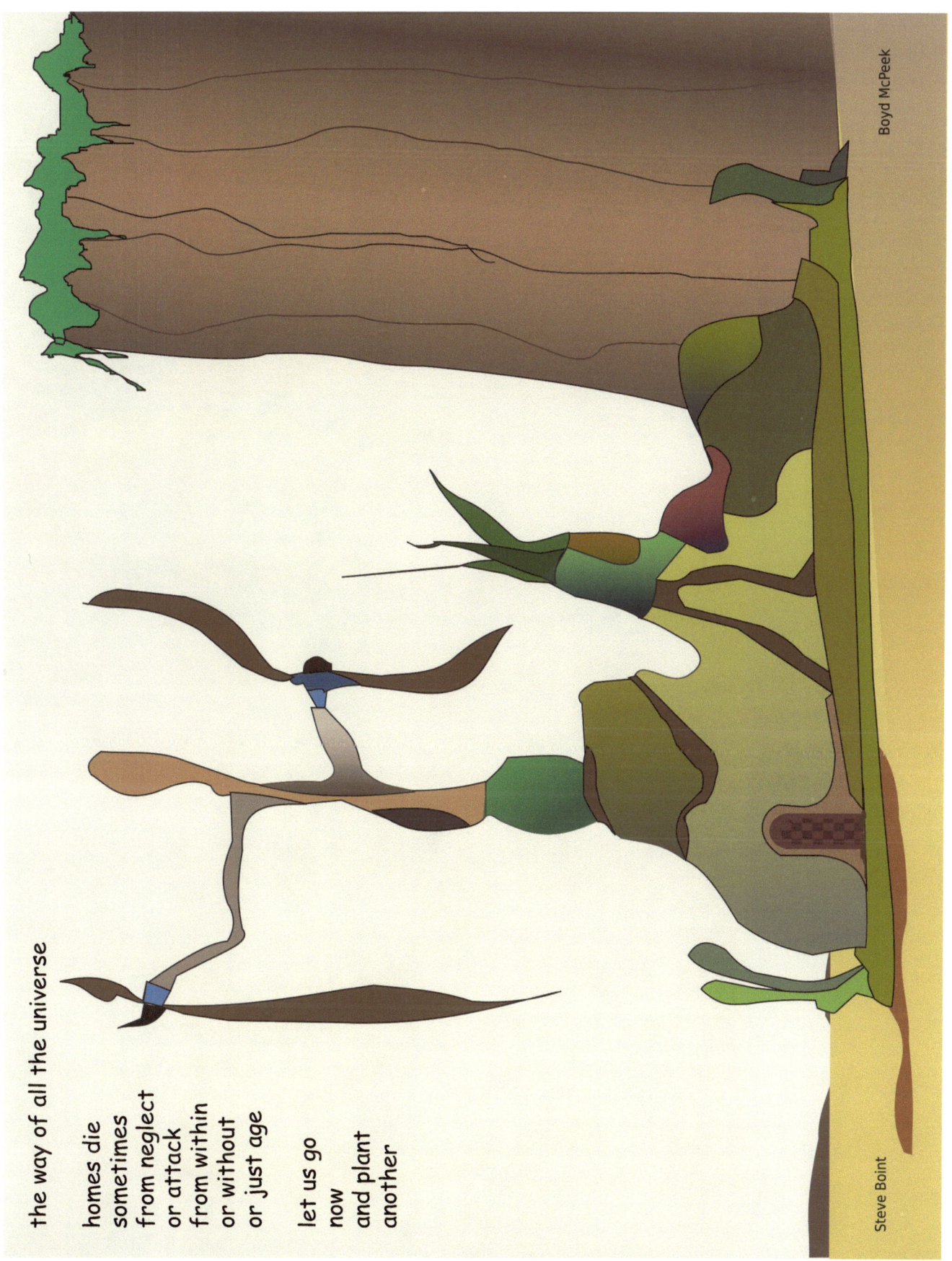

the way of all the universe

homes die
sometimes
from neglect
or attack
from within
or without
or just age

let us go
now
and plant
another

Steve Boint

Boyd McPeek

39

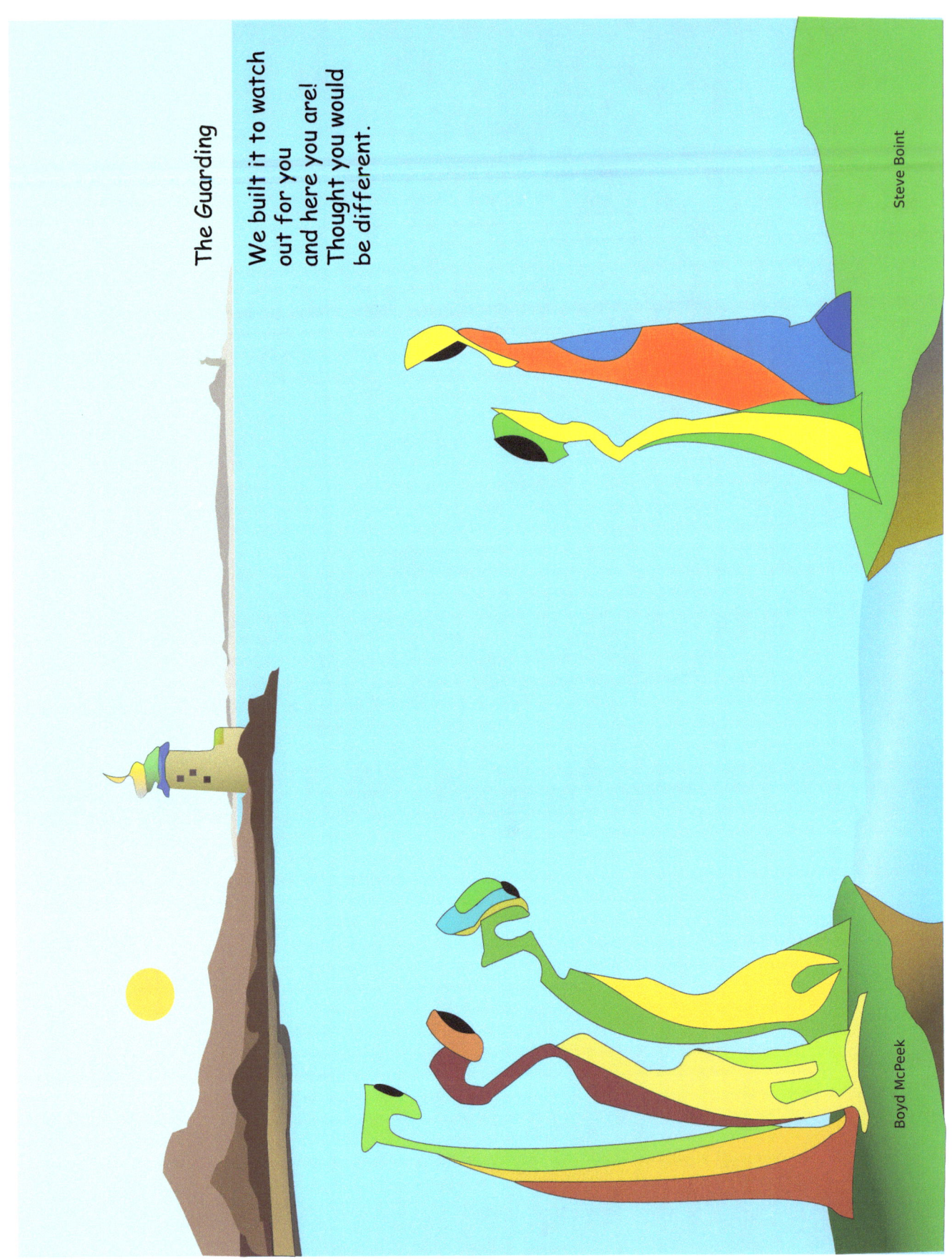

The Guarding

We built it to watch
out for you
and here you are!
Thought you would
be different.

Steve Boint

Boyd McPeek

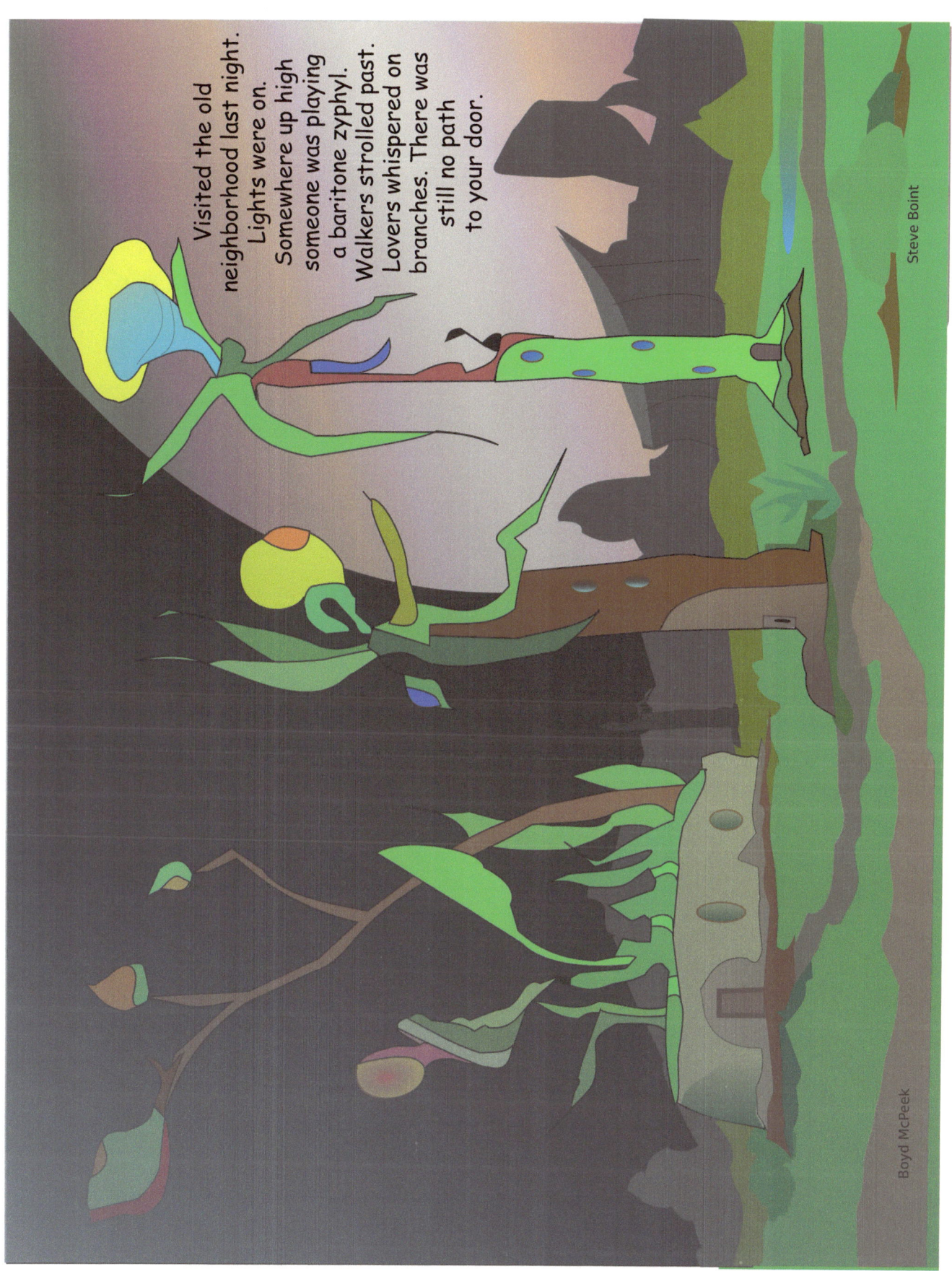

Visited the old neighborhood last night. Lights were on. Somewhere up high someone was playing a baritone zyphyl. Walkers strolled past. Lovers whispered on branches. There was still no path to your door.

Steve Boint

Boyd McPeek

41

and a home.

As wind blew dark beneath methane clouds
and plasma arcs rivaled the moon,
on the edge of vision, strength ebbing to stone,
I found you

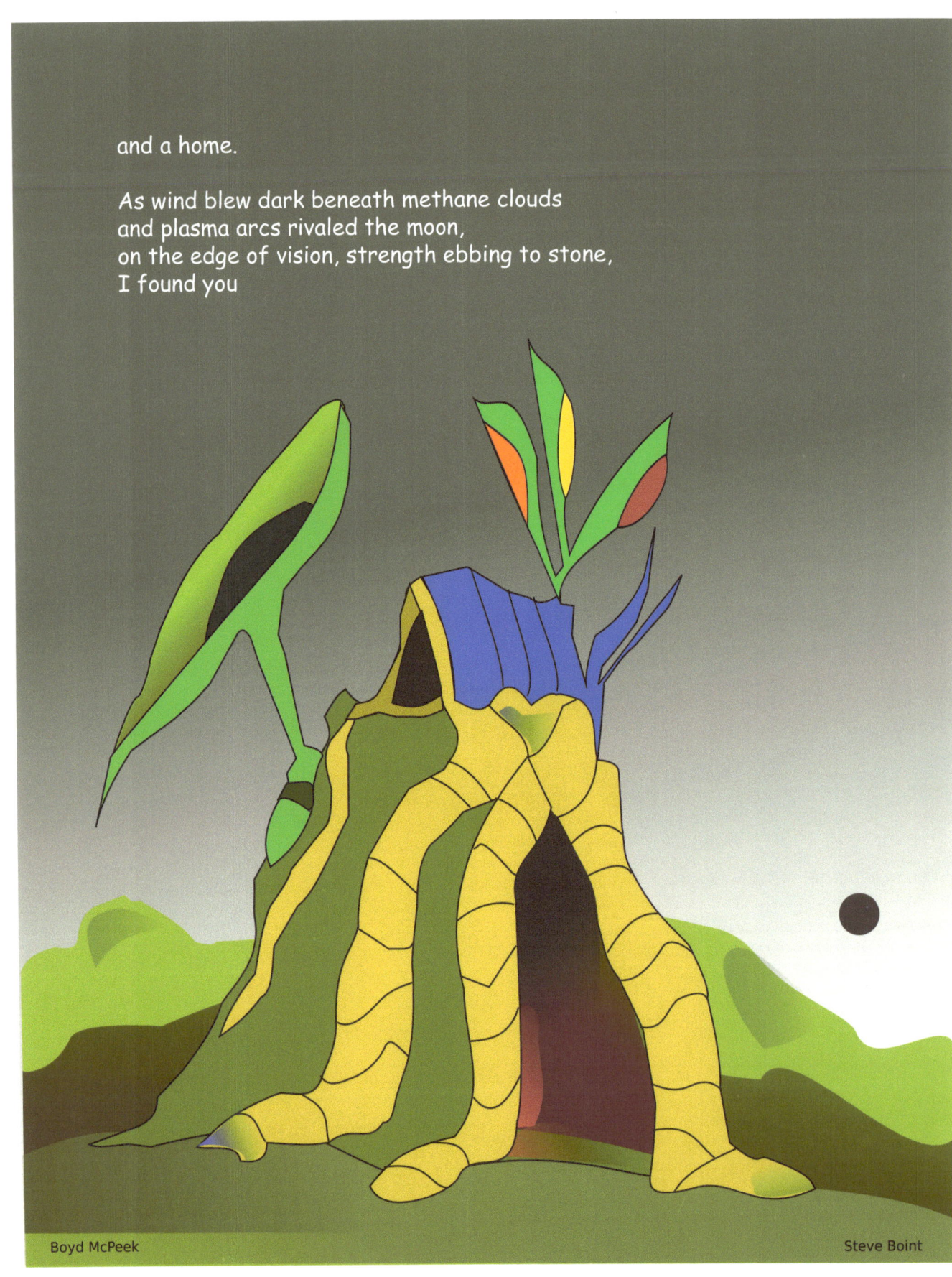

Boyd McPeek

Steve Boint

Through the reflection of Wardington harbor
above schools of squinnow and schrad,
our misadventures done,
leaving the current,
we returned to where it all started
but, this time, as one.

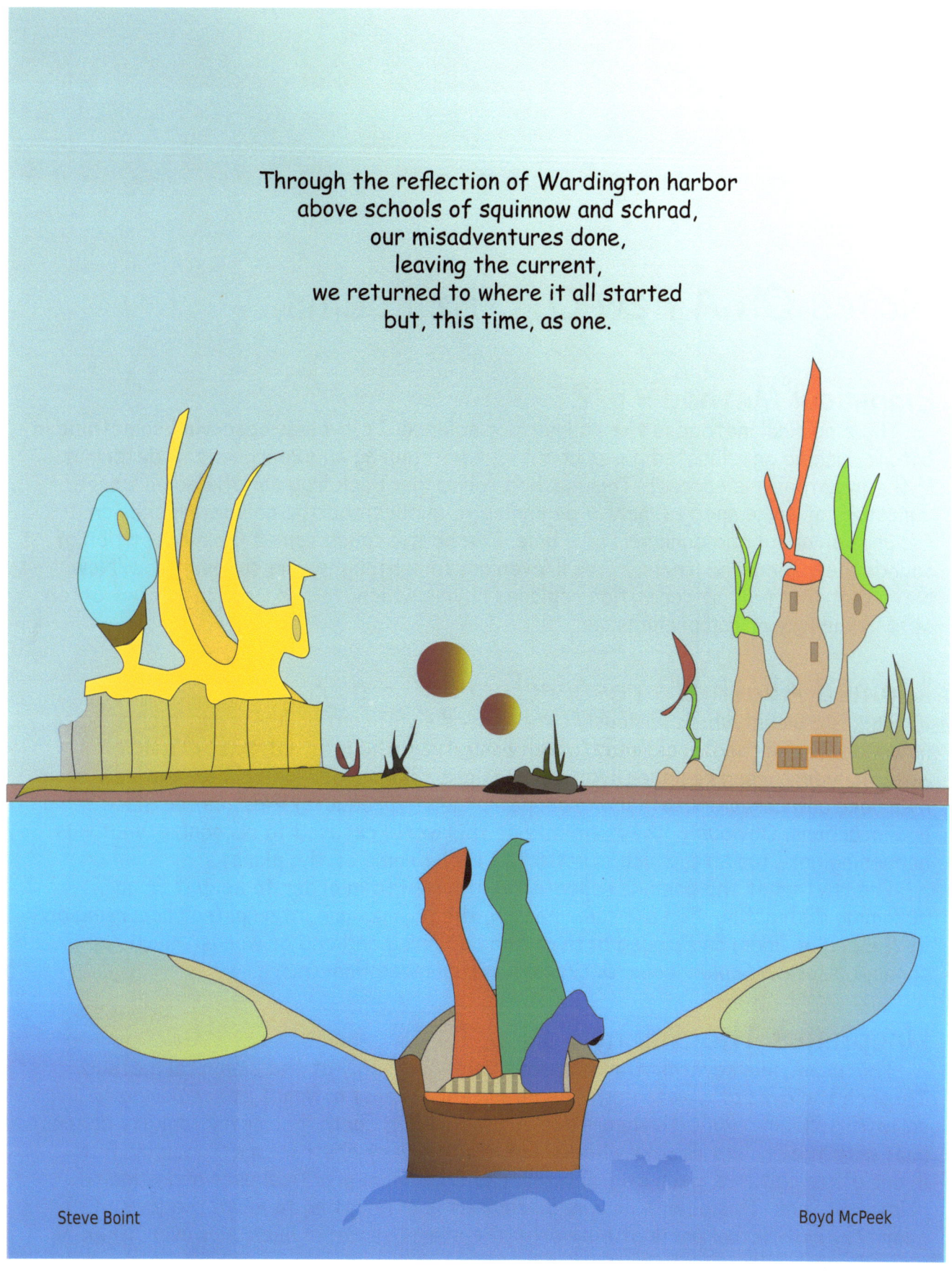

Steve Boint

Boyd McPeek

Notes On A Few Of The Poems

Empirical Method – p. 27

The empirical method is the hallmark of science. It involves observing something in nature, making an educated guess about it, then running an experiment to determine if the hypothesis is correct. This method forms the backdrop for the poem where a member of some species merely beginning to understand the universe makes an assumption about the darkness of a hole. The poetic touch comes from repetition of sounds: deep/underneath/leak/We'll/evening, tonight/light, and spelling: flow/Now. Note that this type of repetition replaces rhyme which, to the modern reader, often gets in the way of comprehension.

"Joined Alioth U's research crew" – p. 7

This is a planet which obviously experienced significant pollution and technologically induced warming: heat, acid seas (which come from the interaction of CO_2 and water), hydrocarbon residue (hydrocarbons are compounds made almost entirely from hydrogen and carbon—in other words, petroleum byproducts). Plastics are made from hydrocarbons. Obviously, the residents of this world refused to recognize what was happening until too late, which is reflected in the name of the planet.

The rhythm of the poem is repeatedly interrupted in order to keep it from becoming distracting. For the same reason, the rhymes are internal (not occurring only at the end of lines) and placed both at the beginning and end of words: Alioth/land/sands, U's/crew/Goplandeaux/CO_2/residue/ruins, sea floor/more.

Unophines The Scientific – p. 15

This poem, like several others, spoofs light-heartedly at the empirical method. Through the eyes of a water-dweller, it imagines a first attempt at comparing scientific observation with theoretical geometry. On Earth, geometry took its deepest root with the ancient Greeks who turned it into a very abstract methodology. But in our other cultures, geometry never broke free from practical uses and remained relatively weak. This poem's imagined scientist is attempting to mesh the laws of geometry with actual parts of his world: the stems of water lilies. However, when he pushes his observation to a vantage point new or unusual to his species (above the water), he finds that theory does not blend well with observation: each stem ends in a round leaf.

Puns add to the rhyme and meter. "Geometric schools" puns groupings of fish with the training academies of mathematicians. "That's right, they are wrong" is a word play on "right or wrong". "Muscle opticale" plays with the scientific tendency to use big words where something like "eye" would work. And the name "Unophines" is a play on ancient Greek names (and the tendency, until recently, of intellectual leaders in Europe and America to use Greek or Latin) suggesting the speaker has only one fin.

And Then He Vanished – p. 19

In science, a constant is a number which allows an equation to be written. In the simple equation: $x=y3z$, 3 is a constant and shows that z has more of an effect in determining x than does y.

When writing this poem, I was thinking of Darwin's statement which I believe is in *The Descent of Man*, "Ignorance more frequently begets confidence than does knowledge: it is those who know little, not those who know much, who so positively assert that this or that problem will never be solved by science." And I remember a study which showed that eyewitnesses to crimes usually are wrong in their memories and the more certain they are of specific details, the more likely they are to be wrong. I got to wondering about the effect on society if someone could actually quantify the error that comes with human certainty.

Met A Soliptian Once – p. 33

Solipsism is the philosophical teaching that nothing exists except for you, unless it is true, in which case nothing exists except for me. This poem plays with the difficulties inherent in this philosophy by positing a species of solipsists.

Silverstein Promontory – p. 3

If you haven't already, you really should read Shel Silverstein's *Where the Sidewalk Ends*.

Steve Boint
May, 2014

My Drawing Technique

It's all about lines . . . doodles using one continuous line. The line flowing around the page makes shapes in the spaces it encloses. The shapes may be plants, animals, buildings, spaceships or nothing at all. When a shape looks like something, I add more lines.

Curved lines connecting the edges of narrow shapes give a tubular look like a tree branch. Repeating segments created by the lines are shaded in alternating colors when I get to the coloring step. An arched line creates half-moon segments for bright colors in the final drawing.

If the shape is going to be a structure, I add ovals and rectangles for doors and windows. I may also add whirligigs, wind turbines and solar leaves. These fanciful features live in other-worldly places not subject to our laws of physics.

Then I add color. I usually use bright, solid colors. My drawing software has a gradient feature that lets me add shading for a three-dimensional effect. These semi-transparent gradients are added over solid colors to create the effect of a watercolor wash. The original lines remain black and are the borders of the shapes. Increasing the weight or thickness of the line emphasizes the shape; decreasing the weight makes it recede into the background. There are other special effects in the software but they look out of place in my drawings so I avoid them.

The final item is the background. Backgrounds are usually very simple in the original sketch, so most of the work is done in the drawing program. Often, blue sky with a slight gradient is the background. However, I've used skies of pink, yellow, green, gray and maroon for a more other-worldly look. Large suns, moons and planets also add to the other-worldly feel.

In summary, the whole process is:
1) doodle a drawing in my sketchbook
2) add lines and simple features
3) scan the doodle into my laptop
4) trace over the scanned image in my drawing program
5) add additional features and color
6) create a background

The drawings are done in a scalable vector graphic (svg) format that allows the image to be re-sized without changing the resolution. The program I use is an open-source program called *Inkscape*. Open-source programs are free programs created and maintained by users like me.

Rocket Girl – p. 17

Rocket Girl is the most whimsical drawing in *Elsewhere*. In this case, the poem came before the picture. I read the first line and set off to find a bruqbruq tree. As it happened, the bleeding hearts were in bloom under the big linden tree in my yard. They made their way into the drawing. Then came the moon turtles which took their look from the full moon. The letters on the bleeding hearts added whimsy and a little definition to the flowers. Orange seas and the morning star completed the allusions to the poem.

The strength of the composition is repetition with variance. The flowers are repeated on both sides of the tree, but they are not mirror images; some are a little larger or at a different angle. This variance in shape catches your eye because you are expecting the flowers to be uniform. If they were uniform the picture would be less interesting.

The two main branches could have been a simple V-shape, but instead they curve to the right and then back to the left. They are similar but not identical. Placing the moon turtles high and low on either side of the tree balances the negative spaces that are the pieces of sky outlined by the branches. There are a couple of small shapes that fit the pattern as well. See if you can find those.

With the composition figured out, the colors were pretty easy to add. The pink and red of the bleeding hearts and the orange seas were the anchors. The other colors had to complement the main colors without attracting too much attention. I chose greens and browns because they are subdued and suggest earth and vegetation.

If I said I thought about all that when I drew the picture, I would be lying. I didn't recognize those things until I wrote this. I just knew that this version of the dozen or so versions I drew had something the others didn't.

Silverstein Promontory – p. 3

This drawing is an example of my basic style. The curving S shape was part of a larger doodle. I liked the S shape, so I extracted it to stand on its own. The short lines on one section of the S create segments that get smaller towards the top. This creates depth. Alternating colors on these segments add interest by challenging the eye to see if they are all the same. The three vertical segments at the top with small windows increase the depth and emphasize the curvature of the structure.

Notice the red and yellow segments on the right side. There are three segments on the left side as well that are all a single color. Try to imagine how the structure would look if those segments were also red and yellow. With the help of my drawing program, I was able to see how those segments looked with red and yellow. I chose to make them all brown. Why? I found that having red and yellow on the left side seemed to shorten the structure. Many decisions like that are made during the drawing process. I am not thinking about composition rules when this happens. My brain is using built-in rules and simply tells me what looks good and what doesn't.

"She's the one made the Blinding Run" – p. 11

When I was younger I read a lot of science fiction and fantasy and was fascinated by the strange worlds and complex life forms I encountered. I actually read the *Lord of the Rings* trilogy before it became a blockbuster movie series. Hobbits and underground houses in the Shire were great stuff for the imagination.

This drawing, however, was more influenced by Frank Herbert's *Dune*. I envisioned an alien adapted to living on a hot desert planet circling a blazing sun. It started as a doodle with swoopy lines. When I saw an alien in the lines, I added solid black areas to emphasize the eyes, mask, wrists and legs. Light red gradients like watercolor washes accentuate the roundness of arms and hips. The long arms, large head and wide shoulders and hips create a powerful-looking body.

Originally, the lower legs looked like birds' legs with reversed knee joints. When I updated the drawing, I replaced the legs with springy-looking android legs like those used by amputee runners. I think this gives the alien a little more swagger.

The background was inspired by the South Dakota Badlands in July. The eroded peaks have bands of pink and gray sediment that are distinctive to the Badlands and give the drawing an other-worldly look.

From An Ancient On Zenphar – p. 1

From An Ancient on Zenphar is a drawing inspired by the poem. It is different because I actually knew what I wanted to achieve before I started drawing. I wanted a windy, sunny day and I wanted to show how the Ancient might try to go elsewhere.

I used yellow, green and tan tones for a warm look. The landscape is layered with horizontal areas leading to the vegetation in the rear. The vegetation was drawn with rapid, slanting strokes of the computer mouse to get a wind-blown look. The long, slim cloud also suggests horizontal movement from the wind. The color of the cloud is echoed in the color of the rock in the mid ground and the door handle on the capsule. All of the background objects are drawn without borders for a hazy look. The capsule and parachute are drawn with borders to make them stand out.

So, how does the Ancient go elsewhere? I watched a video of a lunatic riding a balloon so high he could see the edge of space. Then he jumped out! If there are people bold enough to do that, then the Ancient could be bold enough to hitch a homemade space capsule to a parachute and cast his fate to the wind. Is the modest parachute big enough to yank the capsule off the ground? See if you can find the answer in the book.

Learn – p. 12

Imagine if you planted a seed and a house grew. And, the leaves growing out of the roof were also solar collectors. Instead of removing trees to build a house, you grow a house that is a tree; a tree that provides shade and protection from the elements in exchange for protection from developers. There are about sixteen drawings in *Elsewhere* that are loosely based on this "planthouse" concept. Besides colorful leaves growing from the roof, some structures have wind turbines, solar leaves and objects of unknown use.

Learn is the best example of a planthouse in *Elsewhere*. It has doors, windows, a dormer, wind turbine and a solar leaf. I doodled the organic shape of the house first and then added the other features. The wide brown lines create curved organic shapes. Simple gradients in several places add roundness and depth. The three green objects on the roof increase in size and height from right to left. This pattern follows the shape of the roof which also increases in height from right to left. The yellow, open flower and the solar leaf lean to the right. The unopened yellow flower and the wind turbine lean to the left for balance. The narrow green leaves also show the pattern of repetition with variance that I described earlier.

The overall effect of the composition is whimsical, but it reflects my interest in alternative architecture, energy and the environment. If the wind is steady and the sunshine strong, this off-the-grid planthouse is energy self-sufficient.

People have told me that my drawings look like places they would like to visit. *Elsewhere* is a collection of imaginary destinations for you. I hope you enjoyed the journey.

Boyd McPeek
April, 2014